WATCH FOR TRAMS

WATCH FOR TRAMS

Colin Jones

Kangaroo Press

My mother had two aunts who were so fat that it was a commonplace in the family that they both took up two seats on the tram. To the conductors who only charged them one fare each, this book is dedicated.

Picture from previous page:
Trial trip of the George Street tramway, November 1899—Lord Beauchamp, Governor of New South Wales, is in the top hat, and on his left is Mr R. Hickson, commissioner and engineer in chief of Roads, Bridges and Sewerage. On his right is Mr E. O'Sullivan, secretary for Public Works. *(National Library)*

Cover design by Darian Causby showing:
(*Top left*) Bendigo crossbench car restored to 1913 state. (*D. Robertson*)
(*Top right*) R1-class tram, Sydney Museum. (*C. Jones*)
(*Bottom left*) Tram at Glenelg. (*C. Jones*)
(*Bottom right*) Elizabeth Street with Watch for Trams sign. (*C. Jones*)
(Back cover) Tram at Victoria Bridge, with decorations for the Royal Visit, 1954. (*M. Jones*)

Whilst every effort has been made to locate and acknowledge the owners of the photographs used in this book, due to the passage of time, this has not always been possible.

First published in 1993 by Kangaroo Press Pty Ltd
3 Whitehall Road Kenthurst NSW 2156
PO Box 6125 Dural Delivery Centre NSW 2158 Australia
Typeset by G.T. Setters Pty Limited
Printed in Hong Kong through Independent Book Manufacturers

ISBN 0 86417 544 2

Contents

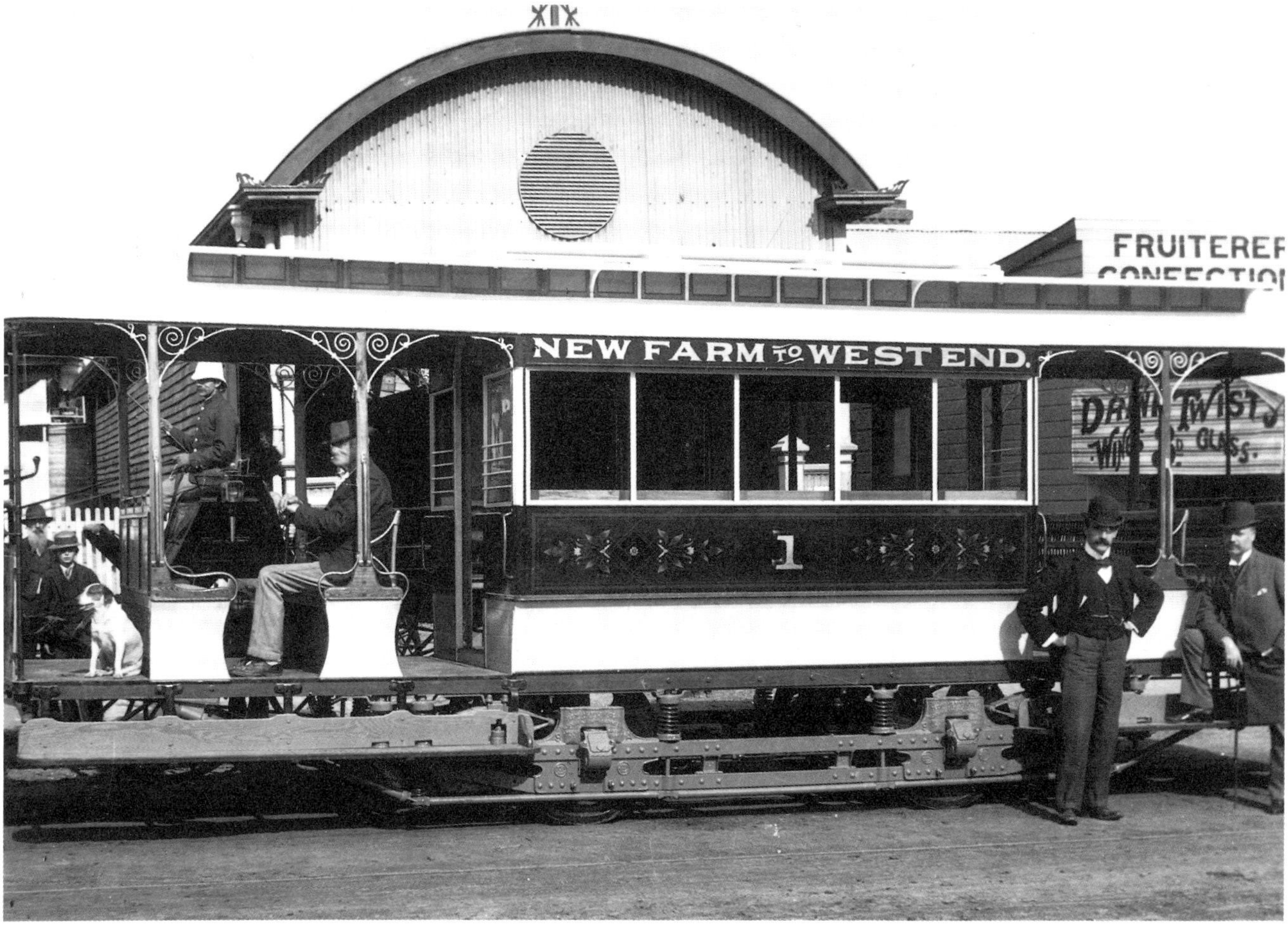

Brisbane horse tram and prototype electric tram—portraits were done of all the types of Brisbane trams in 1896. The dog obviously had to be included with the old horse tram as well as the new electric tram. *(Brisbane City Council)*

Introduction

There was in Brisbane when I was young, no conception at all that trams were not a permanent feature of the city. We had seen new tracks laid near our home, and new streamlined trams that seemed to us like the acme of modernity. The limits of the city were set at the tram terminuses, which determined the boundary between the urbane and the slightly rustic. In fact the Japanese word for a tramcar includes the word which normally indicates a city. Coming back from the south coast you knew you were in Brisbane when you saw the tram at Mount Gravatt.

Along with trams in Brisbane were trolley buses. These were not widespread, but they demonstrated a wondrous silence as they slid in to the kerb in Edward Street. Most of my travelling was on the train, the grimy but serviceable servant of the suburbs; the locomotives with their chime whistles and their cylinders steaming; the crossbench wooden carriages filling with smoke through an open window in Central Station tunnel; and afternoons under the great arch of the station roof. I rarely travelled on the motor buses. They were a poor substitute. One I can recall even failed to tackle the grade on our hill, and all the passengers had to get out and walk. But the trams: they were one of the unconsidered staples of life, regular and predictable. I remember on rainy days how the water beat past the canvas blinds on the old trams and you had to keep your raincoat close about you; or on a summer day sitting in the breeze in the open section of a drop-centre. Smoking was allowed in the rear half of the trams, and this resulted in a considerable degree of division of the sexes — women in the front and men in the back. I took my first girl out to the pictures on the tram — the films now forgotten but the girl remembered.

It was the very oddity of the trams that first struck me in Sydney — some had doors all along the side.

When I came to live in Melbourne, the trams — reliable, crowded, frequent — confirmed a view that they were one of the things that gave proper character to a city. The Melbourne trams were big, and like queens they paraded along the broad streets. They seemed to be a reassurance that the city still stood for the traditional values. To go by their fleet numbers, there were more of them than there were hymns in the hymn-book. As a train traveller I would often regret the descent to unpredictable service, the slashed seats, the graffiti and the occasional leaking roof and, returning to the trams as a regular commuter, the contrast was considerable. The Melbourne trams remained smart and clean, the conductors sociable, the services well-maintained. In the morning and the evening there were the familiar faces behind the newspapers, and at lunchtime the crowds of office workers coming two or three stops to the city department stores or the smart boutiques. Solid and well-designed, the trams seemed sometimes never to have aged, until seen beside the sleek products of modern technology.

As the number of new trams on the road increases, so, it seems, does the nostalgia for the old days. I am not immune, having been born within the sound of the trams in a city that has them no more. Much to the bemusement of my wife, I still navigate around Brisbane by the tram routes, and I am not the only one. Writing in *The Australian Magazine* of 12 December 1992, David Malouf said, 'The old tram routes that once mapped the city still hold it in an invisible net'.

This book is written by an unashamed partisan of the trams. They are civilised and civilising. A city without trams is the poorer, as Brisbane has found. Sydney would like its trams again if it could afford them. Wherever I go in the world there is always someone who will say, 'We should never have got rid of the trams'. In Melbourne they are still there; one after the other down the great boulevard of St Kilda Road, and still green to match the trees; queueing up at the busy city stops in Bourke Street; shining in the dark streets on rainy nights; a tram to the beach, a tram to the city, a tram to the football; the symbol of Melbourne, the necessity of urban life.

The Pitt Street tram at Hunter Street, one of only two known photographs. *(C. Jones collection)*

The horses break into a spirited gallop as they pull a tram in Batavia in 1872. In this romanticised view, the Dutchman is seen pointing out the value of the tramway's civilising influence to the local population. *(Illustrated Australian News)*

1

The American Invention

In olden times, people who wanted to get around in cities kept a carriage, or they walked. Cities were not large physically, and frequently they were constrained by their walls and fortifications, so this caused no real inconvenience. From the middle of the seventeenth century the rising middle classes in London could hire a hackney-carriage, but demand for true public transport in towns did not come until much later. In France, in 1825, a gentleman named Baudry was the proprietor of some hot water baths, and to attract people to their rather suburban location, just outside the town of Nantes, he instituted a line of public carriages. The name he gave to this new type of vehicle derived from the shop sign of a hatter named Omnes who, to persuade the public at large to buy his products, had painted in large letters, 'Omnes Omnibus', (or 'Omnes Products for Everyone'). The new carriage line was for everybody and so Baudry named them 'omnibuses'. The baths failed to prosper, but the omnibuses proved very popular, and during the 1830s the idea spread to Paris, Lyons, Dresden and London, and across the Atlantic to New York, Philadelphia and Boston. New York had 100 omnibuses in 1835, while competition between proprietors had become so anarchic in London by 1832 that the Stage Carriage Act was passed to allow the licensing of drivers and conductors. Omnibuses were popular, but they were soon to have a rival, the tram.

The idea of using rails on which to run vehicles went back to the seventeenth century, where, in mining areas, 'tramroads' were constructed for carrying the ore. The word 'tram' comes from the low German 'Traam', a balk or beam, first applied to the frames of the small mining trucks and later to the tracks on which they ran. The first tramroad with iron rails was built in 1776, and from then on it was a case of steady development which saw the world's first passenger-carrying railway, in Wales, in 1807. Soon there were steam locomotives available, and by 1825 the old idea of the tramroad had been transformed into the modern idea of the railway. By the 1830s, in London, a suburban railway could make things very difficult for a rival omnibus line.

The Americans now enter the picture with what must have seemed at first to be a very small innovation, the building of a railway on the public streets of New York. A man named John Mason was responsible for the New York and Harlem Railroad, whose tracks extended down the broad reaches of Fourth Avenue and the Bowery. The world's first tram, modelled after the style of a contemporary railway carriage, was built by a man who was to become famous for the building of tramcars, John Stephenson, and it was pulled on its first journey behind a team of smart grey horses on 14 November 1832. The idea was initially slow to spread, probably because the whole idea of public transport in towns was very new, but by the end of the 1850s there were trams in the largest United States cities — New York, New Orleans, Brooklyn, Boston, Philadelphia, Baltimore, Cincinnati, Pittsburgh and Chicago — and the first tramway had opened in Paris, where, appropriately, it was called 'le chemin de fer Americain'.

The tram was everything the omnibus was not. It was faster, smoother, quieter, roomier, and safer and cheaper to operate. It had brakes, and a single horse could pull a tram of double the weight of an omnibus. As a result, fares could be lower. In New York, with trams on five of the major thoroughfares, the omnibuses had a hard time of it. Steam engines were provided to haul some New York trams as early as 1835.

The man who introduced the tram to England was an archetype of the hustling American entrepreneur. Then only 31 years of age, Boston-born George Francis Train entered a shipping firm while in his teens and claimed to have ordered the building of the famous clipper *Flying Cloud*. By the age of 24 he was in Melbourne, where he imported the latest American-designed Concord coaches and provided the financial backing for Freeman Cobb to start his nationwide network of stage coaches. Back in Boston a few years later he was financing the construction of railroads, and in 1860 opened the first tramway in England, at Birkenhead, across the river from Liverpool. In the following year he opened a line in London. It was Train's patents which were chosen when the first tramway in Australia was built, in Sydney, in 1861.

The first Australian tramway had its genesis in the unfortunate location of the Sydney railway terminal, in 1855, at Redfern, some distance from the centre of the city and, more importantly, some distance from the docks. By 1858, pressure was being exerted for an extension to be built, in the form of a tramway, from Redfern through to Circular Quay. By early 1861, when the bill for the construction of the tramway was before the colonial parliament, the proprietors of businesses in Pitt Street, along which it was to run, were petitioning the House in its favour. Sixteen months later they had changed their tune.

The opening day, 23 December 1861, was a great success. The two tramcars were a great novelty. Much larger than their rival omnibuses, they were gaily painted in yellow and emblazoned with their names, *Old England* and *Young Australia*, surmounted with the lion of England and the eagle of America, supporting the motto, 'Unity is the Strength of Nations'. The timetable provided that the trams met each train, which gave them five return trips per day and one on Sundays. The fare was 3 *d.*, against the equivalent omnibus fare of 4 *d.* The relative value of this fare may be judged against the tram conductor's wage of 8 *s.* (that is, 32 fares) per day. The *Sydney Morning Herald* noted that 'the motion of the car is extremely easy and comfortable, and passengers accustomed to the rattling and jolting of the 'buses, will appreciate the means now afforded of entirely escaping from those annoyances'.[1] Each tram could seat 30 inside, 30 on the roof and as many could stand as could squeeze aboard. Thus the traveller coming from Liverpool in the train could continue his journey in the tram and, should he be going so far, he would find the smart paddle-steamer *Phantom* waiting at Circular Quay to take him to Manly.

The tram was, however, by no means an unmixed blessing. Its rails stood up above the surface of the street; the gravel surface crumbled beside them; in rain they were muddy and treacherous; and at all times they were a trap for the wheels of carriages and waggons in this very busy thoroughfare. The Pitt Street traders, looking for goods traffic on the tramway which never materialised, saw trade diverted and their land values slipping. By June 1862, 646 property owners had petitioned the government that they 'have suffered and are still suffering serious injury by reason of the ill-designed and ill-constructed piece of machinery known as "The Pitt-street Tramway"'.[2]

A public inquiry revealed that the tramway was of marginal profitability at best and would never repay its capital, that the gradients were too severe for horses to pull loaded goods waggons on it, and that it was regarded as a positive hazard in the middle of the road. Grooved rails, which had been introduced in some parts of the world in 1852, were not considered a

First tram in Birkenhead. *(Illustrated London News)*

solution as the grooves would just fill up with stones. It was also noted that Train's tramways were being pulled up in London for much the same reason. One witness commented that trams were unsuited to Sydney's narrow streets, but would do well in Melbourne, a fact which has been borne out.

The outcome of the inquiry was that the tramway was leased to Mr John Woods, who would run it at more realistic headways and who would be obliged to maintain the road between the tracks and for 46 centimetres on each side. This scarcely suited the tramway's opponents, and their voices were raised as a result of a particularly tragic accident.

By 1864 Isaac Nathan had for 23 years been a great ornament to the Sydney cultural establishment. He had made a name for himself in England before emigrating and in 1847 he had composed the first opera to be written in Australia, *Don John of Austria*. On the afternoon of 15 January 1864 the old gentleman, who had become famous as the 'father of music in Australia', was on his way home on the tram. As he alighted, but before he had properly found his footing, the tram jolted into motion, dragging him against its wheels, where he was killed.

The tramway could please no-one. The green wood of the sleepers warped; in summer the rails, laid without expansion joints, would buckle alarmingly in the hot sun. As J.H. Thomas, an engineer for the Railway Department stated, 'No mortal man could have kept it in repair'.[3] Petition and counter-petition went before parliament until the Pitt Street traders finally had their way and the tramway was closed on 31 December 1866. Within hours the offending tracks were being removed, but John Woods, not to be overcome by adversity, resumed his services the following day with four omnibuses.

Australia's first tramway was dead, but the idea was not gone.

2

Iron Rails in Adelaide

During the 1870s Adelaide was a confident city, the third-largest in the colonies and growing at a rate such that, at the end of the decade, it had reached a census population of over 103 000. Beyond the encircling belt of parklands, new suburbs were developing, the most populous of which were Kensington and Norwood. It was not lost on certain people that a person who could provide a better form of public transport than the erratic, expensive and uncomfortable horse buses would stand to make a considerable profit. William Buik and Edwin Smith in particular, both substantial businessmen and active in both colonial and municipal politics, saw that here was a chance for them. While on a visit to Britain in 1872, William Buik had taken note of the success of the horse tramways in London, Glasgow and Edinburgh.[1] These were all new installations and their popularity put Buik in mind of the advantages which would accrue to him if there were a tramway in Adelaide to bring people from the suburbs to the very doors of his Rundle Street premises. In 1875 Buik, Smith and several others floated the Adelaide and Suburban Tramway Company Limited. They then proceeded to seek parliamentary sanction for it.

The whole idea of tramways had matured considerably since the fiasco in Sydney. There was no question of carrying goods on the line, and the rails would be of a modern grooved pattern, set flush with the road surface so as not to interfere with other vehicles. With the available guidance of the British *Metropolitan Street Tramways Act* of 1870, the Adelaide tramway companies would have to maintain the roadway between the tracks and 46 centimetres on each side.[2] The tramway would also be available for compulsory purchase after a period by the government or the Adelaide Corporation. A parliamentary select committee investigated the idea of a tramway during 1876 and refined the legislation under which it was to operate. One aspect, unusual in an Australian tramway, was that, in the generous 40-metre width of King William Street, the two tram tracks were to be laid with their centres no less than 6.4 metres apart.[3] This would have allowed an extension of the Glenelg railway between the tram tracks. Mr B. Boothby, engineer of the Glenelg railway, told the committee:

> I look forward, also, to the time when Adelaide shall have become so populous, that a subway will be made from South-terrace — an underground railway from South-terrace to the back of Government House, and a viaduct across to North Adelaide. It may not be in my day, but I have no doubt it will be done some time.[4]

After a century, Adelaide's underground railway has been proposed several more times but remains a dream. In the event, the space between the tram tracks in King William Street was used in some places for a third tram track, and in others for cab stands.

On a wet and stormy afternoon late in October 1877, the Governor, Sir William Jervois, laid the first rail of Australia's first permanent urban tramway, outside the Norwood Town Hall. The tramway, like all those built in succeeding years in Adelaide, was a true product of capitalist enterprise. When the tracklaying contractor proved to be somewhat dilatory in his work, he was summarily dismissed and the company used its own men to lay the new lines into the city. Twelve tramcars were ordered from that doyen of tramcar builders, John Stephenson of New York. On their arrival they were assembled by the local carriage-building firm of Duncan and Fraser, and although the other tramway companies usually looked to New York for their prototypes, Duncan and Fraser finished up building most of the Adelaide horse trams.

By the end of May 1878 the construction work was finished, and on 10 June the people of Adelaide could ride for the first time on the most up-to-date form of transport in the colonies, a tram. The fare to Kensington was 3 *d*. Public success was instantaneous and services were improved as fast as new horses could be trained, while the company immediately set about building the line to North Adelaide.

Suddenly there was a tramway boom. No fewer than 11 different tramway companies actually started services in the Adelaide, Port Adelaide and Glenelg areas. Two other companies, despite gaining parliamentary approval for their plans, failed to get

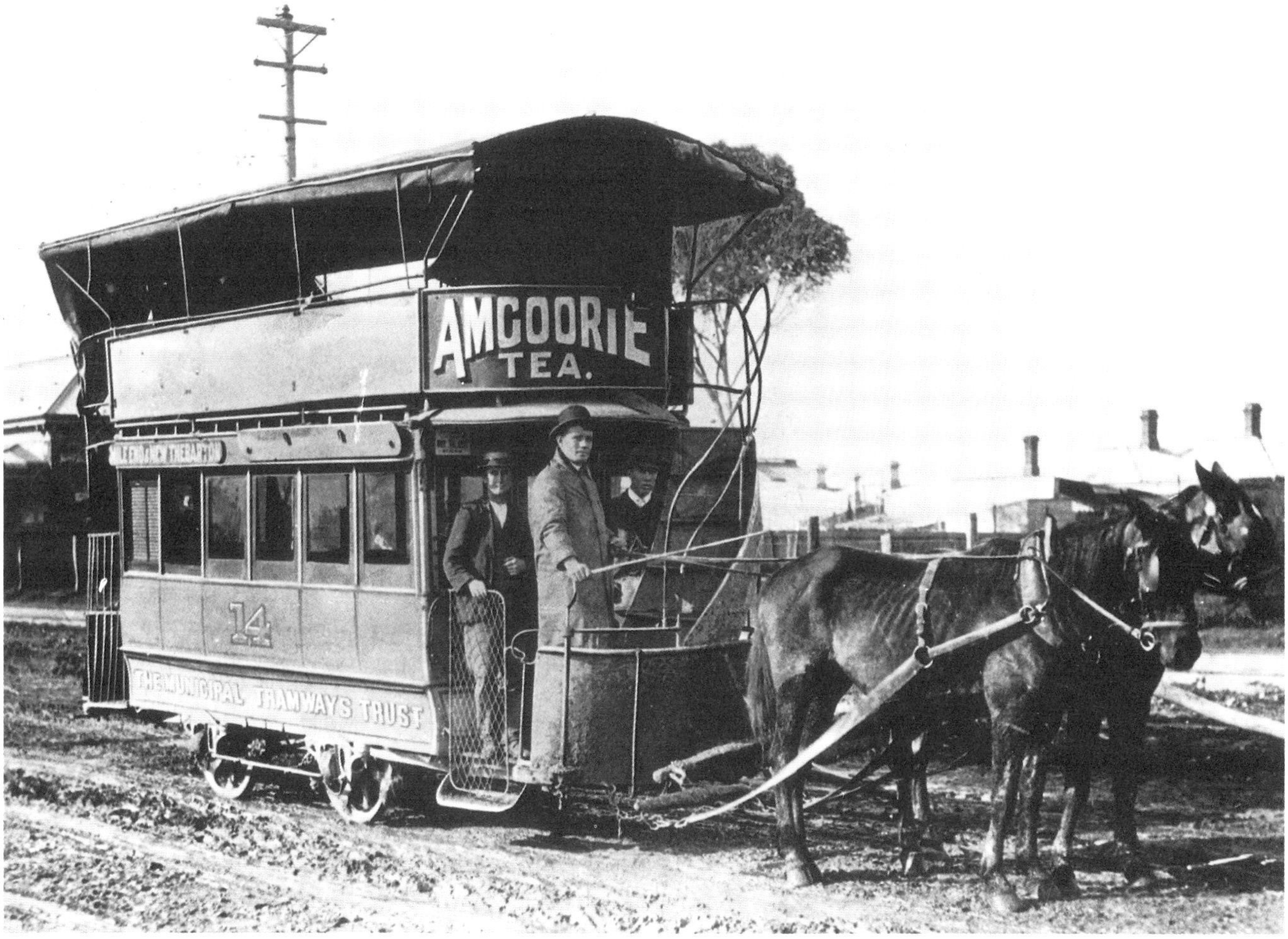

Adelaide horse tram on the Henley Beach line, 1909; definitely a set o' lean horses. *(State Transport Authority)*

as far as starting services, though no doubt some of their shareholders benefited from land speculation along their proposed routes. The South Australian Railways, proprietor of several horse-drawn railway routes in various parts of the colony, contributed an urban tramway in the town of Gawler.

Not all of the companies were rivals, as William Buik and Edwin Smith were principals in two others which served sections of Adelaide outside of the Adelaide and Suburban Tramways Company's franchises. On the other hand, some were deadly rivals. The Adelaide, Prospect, Nailsworth and Enfield Tramway Company's tracks met, but did not connect with, the Adelaide and Suburban system at the Caledonian Hotel in North Adelaide. Owing to the injury claims resulting from the overturning of a tram in 1884 with eight passengers inside and 22 on the top deck, the company was wound up and the line sold more than once. In 1895 the owner, a man named Ragless, fell out with the Adelaide and Suburban company over the fares they charged to take his passengers on to the city. Taking the matter into his own hands, he had Duncan and Fraser build him six carettes — a kind of large omnibus — to take his passengers on the second leg of their journey. As he also undercut the tram fare by a penny, he captured the bulk of the tram passengers, which forced the Adelaide and Suburban company to buy him out.

The Adelaide and Suburban Tramway Company completed its network in 1883 and converted all its single-deck trams to double-deckers, which became a standard for the city. The other ten companies had all commenced their services by that year, though some construction of new lines continued up to 1889. From 1884, Adelaide people had the chance of boarding a tram in North Terrace and finishing up in Paradise. This felicitous suburb name was probably unique in any tramway in the world. Adelaide being a city of churches, people were probably reasonably secure against taking a tram and finishing up in 'the other place'.

Although much larger than omnibuses, the horse trams were, by modern standards, small and light. The largest, which were designed to be pulled by three horses, were 7.3 metres long and could carry 54 people. There were 22 seats inside, another 24 on the 'imperial', as the top deck was at first called, and another eight people could stand on the end platform. For lines of lesser traffic, smaller trams were used, right down to those 'dinkies' whose 4.9 metre length and single decks made them appear like miniatures next to their more capacious brethren. On most trams the

King William Street with trams and buggies. *(State Transport Authority)*

top deck was shaded by a canvas awning, and soldiers with their spiked helmets had to be careful when they rose from their seats lest they damage both the tramway property and their military dignity. One tramway company, afraid that its trams, which ran close to the beach, would be in danger of being blown over by a strong westerly wind, did not provide canopies on the top deck. To have to sit on an open top deck in the rain could be rather a trial, and sometimes the tram driver might pass up spare chaff bags for passengers to hold over their heads.

The trams were brightly painted in yellow and white, but all were liberally covered, in the British manner, by advertising. As they went on their way, the trams silently urged people to buy Amgoorie Tea and Sunlight Soap, to drink Fry's Concentrated Cocoa, or Wolfe's 'The Only Real Schnapps'. Lion Flour, Nestlé's Milk, Union Brand Tobacco, Quaker Oats, Reckitt's Blue, all had their place alongside advertisements for tradespeople, and even election slogans. In capitalist America, advertising was almost never carried on the trams, but in Adelaide it helped eke out what was to become the rather marginal profitability of the tramway companies.

The key to the tramway company's operation was its horses. About ten had to be kept for each tram, as the work was hard, especially starting with a loaded car that could be as much as seven tonnes and hauling this weight up a steady hill. Light medium draught-horses were used and they were preferred about four years old. For about three years, while they were fit enough to work on the trams, they were kept in pairs and each pair was allocated to two drivers. They worked two trips a day and one on Sundays of about 11 kilometres and then returned to their stables, often substantial buildings of stone. For assistance on major hills an extra horse would be used, attached to the tram without its having to stop, by an agile boy who then took the horse down the hill once the grade had been surmounted, to wait for the next car. So many horses, all together in their stables, were easy prey to infectious diseases, which could endanger services if they became widespread. The most famous event of this kind occurred in America in 1872. The Great Epizootic, as it was called, killed thousands of horses and reduced tramway companies in cities such as Boston to having employees haul the cars by hand. Luckily this was never a real problem in Adelaide, though in drought times in the 1890s some horses suffered from eating the wrong type of food. More of a problem was the cost of feeding a large stable of horses, and the disposal of the odorous piles of manure which gathered by each

Busy urban scene in King William Street. The view in the opposite direction is facing page 32. *(postcard)*

Trams in Grenfell Street, waiting to depart for Kensington, 1896. *(S.A. Archives)*

Tram at Mitcham, 1880. *(S.A. Archives)*

depot. The local residents were hardly convinced that the perfumed air had any restorative properties as far as their health was concerned.

A young horse would learn his trade with a pair of more experienced animals on a three-horse tram and then graduate to a smaller two-horse vehicle. If he was unlucky he would find himself working for one of the more impoverished companies, straining to pull the car on his own. At the end of his useful period, perhaps with his hoofs and legs giving trouble, he would be retired to the country for the lighter work of a farm, where often he would give useful service for many years. The only catch for the farmer in buying a tram horse was that it might only start and stop to the ringing of a bell — two bells to start, one bell to stop.

The tram drivers, licensed on an annual basis by the City of Adelaide, were solid dependable men, though often not without a wry sense of humour. The conductors, on the other hand, were boys straight from school, between the ages of 13 and 17 and universally known as 'tram boys'. The usual shifts for the tram crews were from 5.45 a.m. to 3.45 p.m., or from 3.45 p.m. to 12.30 a.m., and for this an experienced driver was paid £2 10*s*. 0*d*. per week and the conductor 15 *s*. The driver was in charge on the tram, but his example was not considered enough to kerb the larrikin element which might inevitably surface with the tram boys. As a result, the tramway company's rules for their behaviour contained some real gems.

> The Conductor must not allow any boys on the back platform, nor is he to ride on the back platform of any car of which he is not conductor.
>
> The Conductor must always be civil and polite to passengers and in no case use bad language or call out to any other conductor on the road while passing.
>
> Conductors may sit on the fourth step of the stairs with their feet on the second step while travelling, but must not sit on the dash, or lean against the gates.
>
> Conductors are not allowed to read while travelling.
>
> No conductor is allowed to play on the cars, nor to throw stones, or play any game that is prohibited on the Company's premises.

Almost from these rules alone, the character of the boys may be surmised. Likewise the rules for drivers:

> Smoking is strictly prohibited while driving, and the use of intoxicating liquors will be sufficient cause for discharge.
>
> Drivers must not allow any unauthorised persons to drive their horses or cars to collide with other horses or cars, or any other vehicle, while the car they are driving is in motion; must take no chance of any person, carriage or wagon getting out of the way, but must act with caution; it will be no excuse to say that you thought something; what we require is that you stop and take no risks.[5]

At their official maximum speed of 13 kilometres per hour, the trams were appropriate for their leisurely times. There were no set stopping places, but a ring on the bell would stop the tram wherever a passenger wanted, perhaps even stopping individually for houses next door to each other. It was not unknown for some trams on an hourly schedule in the outer suburbs to stop and wait for someone who was running late, or even while they ran back to their house for something they had forgotten. So much were they a part of the community that the story was told of a woman who wished to visit a friend in Walkerville stopping the Walkerville tram in King William Street to ask the driver if he knew whether her friend was at home. After a moment's thought, the driver replied that she

Trams and cabs waiting for passengers. *(S.A. Archives)*

was not, as he had brought her into town on his last trip. One dear old lady always rode free. She had an orchard at the Mitcham terminus, from which the tram crews were always free to help themselves. When she rode on the trams she might quietly murmur 'Peaches' to the conductor, but the word was not quite so effective with the ticket inspector.

On the long run out to Henley Beach the trams would perform a number of homely functions such as delivering the newspapers (the conductor might only need to pass them over to a smiling well-trained dog to be taken home) or taking shopping orders. The takings of shops along the line might be given to the conductor to bank, so he would certainly earn his tips with the running around he had to do while the tram lay over at the terminus in King William Street. All of this, of course, brought the trams very close to the community that they served.

The last car for Burnside left the city at 9.15 p.m., but for a guaranteed 2*s*. 6*d*. in fares, the company would run the last Marryatville car out to Burnside. As a result, people in Burnside who wished to visit the theatre would make sure that they all went on the same night. Late-night trams were often referred to as 'drunks' specials' and no nice girl would travel on them unescorted. The Magill tram, which turned a very sharp corner out of Kent Terrace, was always a favourite with its bibulous passengers, who would endeavour to derail it as it went around, to have the fun of putting it back on the line.

The Adelaide and Suburban Tramway Company kept itself in reasonable financial condition, but some of the other companies never paid a dividend. Adelaide's boom of the early 1880s was short-lived, and as the years progressed the tramways became dilapidated and unreliable. By the mid-1890s, horse omnibuses had reappeared in competition with the trams, but in their depressed circumstances, nothing could be done. Even when the tramways were established it was realised that there were better forms of motive power available than horses. Two companies actually started in 1879 with steam tram motors, but these proved not to be a success in the circumstances. The other experiment was with electricity.

In 1888 the Australian Electric Tramway company was formed to exploit a French patent for trams powered by electric batteries. The first trials of a battery-powered electric tram were made in Sydney in June, and later in Melbourne and Ballarat. In January 1889 the same type of electric tram was tried in Adelaide, on the run to Henley Beach. Although it was a success, it was not a sufficiently convincing demonstration to lead to any subsequent investment by the tramway companies. Only in Bendigo, in Victoria, was a full-scale tramway system set up with battery power, and it was an abject failure. Like the legendary Rolls Cnardley motor car, which rolls down the hill but can hardly get up the next one, Bendigo's battery trams stalled on grades, with smoke coming out of their motors, and often ran out of power long before reaching the terminus. They were tolerated for only a few months before being replaced by the infinitely more reliable steam trams. Sydney was the only system to make a success, if a modest one, of a battery tram, with one vehicle of the type running for just over a year in the mid-1890s.

The later years in Adelaide brought a certain amount of sympathy for the overtaxed horses and are typified by a contemporary joke. What is the difference between the Adelaide trams and the Adelaide street lights? One has a set o' lean horses, and the other has acetylene lamps![6]

By the early years of the twentieth century, Adelaide, with its city-wide system of obsolete horse trams, had fallen behind the rest of the country. None of the existing companies could face the cost of re-equipping with modern electric technology, and so most were bought by the South Australian government for a total figure of £280 372 18*s*. 4*d*. Apart from the track and buildings, the six companies' assets amounted to 162 trams, 6 carettes, 5 wagonettes, 11 omnibuses and 1056 horses.

Author at the controller, Brisbane Tramway Museum. *(W. Gibson)*

Tram on the causeway, Victor Harbor. *C. Jones)*

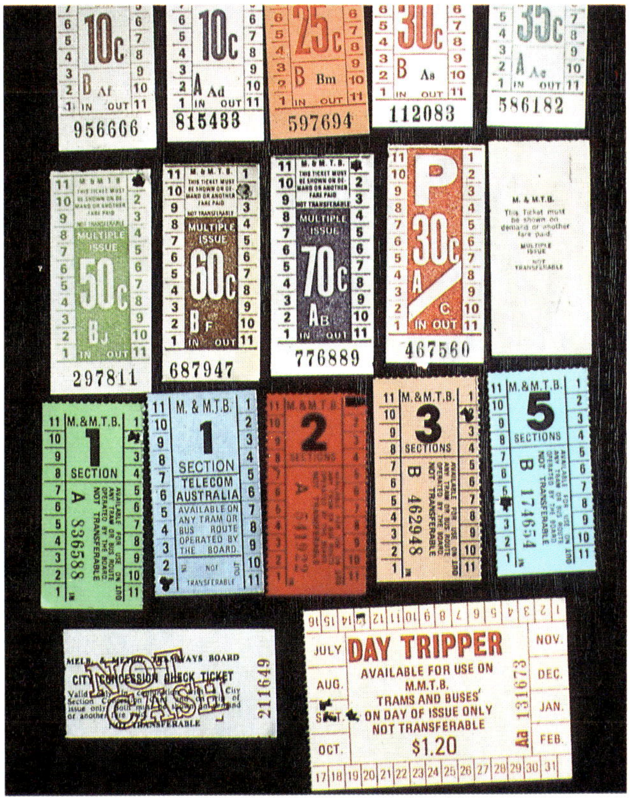

Melbourne and Brisbane tram tickets. Brisbane always advertised Tritton's furniture store on the reverse side. *(C. Jones collection)*

Straight from the tram to the sand; holiday time at Henley Beach. *(postcard)*

Melbourne Zoo horse tram replica at Kilmore. *(C. Jones)*

3

Steam in the Streets

For almost 30 years after the opening of Sydney's first railway, the citizens of the capital looked in vain for the building of extensions in the city and suburban area. In obedience to political forces, the lines reached out west to recapture the Riverina from the rival colony of Victoria. The city had to make do with the ubiquitous omnibus — one every three minutes and mind the stairs; no more than 15 people please.

Through the 1870s, as Sydney's population rose towards its 1881 Census figure of 224 200, pressure began to mount for the reintroduction of tramways. In 1873 Jorgen Larsen, who had patented a particular type of grooved tramway rail, attempted to gain parliamentary approval for a horse tramway, but although reports from England, Europe and America indicated that tramways were becoming a great success, the memories of the unfortunate Pitt Street line were too recent and the idea failed.

The Railway Department badly needed the city railway. When John Whitton, the chief engineer, designed a new station building for the Redfern terminal, he left an arch facing Sydney so the line could be extended. Now he proposed a grand terminal station in Hyde Park with a goods line to Circular Quay, or alternatively, a terminal at Hunter and Castlereagh Streets. These plans would have required the purchase and demolition of much of the urban fabric of central Sydney, including Francis Greenway's St James's Church, and the public rejected them conclusively. The public also had a need, and that was for better transport in the city. In his evidence before the parliamentary committee investigating a new proposal put forward by the Sydney Tramway and Omnibus Company, Robert Massie, a stock agent, said:

> I look upon travelling in a Waverley 'bus as purgatory. I conceive that we have to undergo in a week so many hours of intense misery. It is one of the worst punishments a man can undergo to have to travel by them. As far as my experience goes, I would sooner use a tram car than any conveyance I know of.[1]

John Young, chairman of the company, which already had a virtual monopoly of omnibus services in Sydney, underlined the point when he said, 'There is scarcely a city with 3000 inhabitants in any part of Europe or America without tramways'.[2]

The year was 1878 and the 9227 signatures on petitions to parliament in favour of the proposed tramways legislation proved that the time for trams had come. In the end, though, it was the solid Yorkshire engineer John Whitton who was to get his way, and not John Young. While rival city tramway and railway proposals floundered, Sydney was preparing to stage the Great International Exhibition. On a two-hectare site in the Botanic Gardens, the great Garden Palace was arising, with its dome of wood and glass and its fretted towers. The exhibition was due to open in the middle of September 1879 and unless Sydney could provide adequate public transport from the railway to the Garden Palace, it would be shamed in the eyes of the world. A tramway there had to be, and the government would provide it.

Preparations were pushed ahead swiftly for a line that would run from the forecourt of the railway terminal via Elizabeth Street to a convenient terminus at the corner of Elizabeth and Hunter Streets. Although the line was intended to be temporary, and to be closed at the end of the Exhibition in April 1880, it was well equipped with four steam tram motors and six double-decked trailer cars. These demonstrated the latest in American technology. The steam tram motors were a sturdy design from the Baldwin locomotive works of Philadelphia, little four-wheeled steam locomotives, disguised behind a shell of painted and polished timer and glass to resemble, to the view of the skittish horses, an ordinary tramcar. The wheels, connecting rods and other gear were hidden behind hinged flaps. The cars, built to the design of the noted Philadelphia company of J. G. Brill, seated 60 on the lower deck and 30 on the upper. Passengers were protected from the weather, and from flying smuts from the chimneys of the motors, by canvas blinds and awnings. It was estimated that one tram motor could do the work of 16 horses, and at little more than half the cost. The equipment left New York aboard the *Dryad* on the same day that tracklaying began in Pitt Street outside Christ Church St Laurence, but

Trams nudge the footpath on the Phillip Street corner. Typically, someone has planted a pole right on the edge. *(C. Jones collection)*

the railway authorities, nervous that their steam stock would not arrive in time, ordered two horse tramcars from the local firm of Hudson Bros.

The *Dryad* was three weeks overdue; the exhibition was almost ready; visitors would be pouring into Sydney. Then finally all was well and the railway staff hurried to assemble and test their new trams. They were not quite in time. Like the ghost of the old Pitt Street tramway, two horse trams commenced running on 16 September 1879, the day before the opening of the Exhibition. Twelve days later the people of Sydney could ride on the first of their new steam trams.

They were a spectacular success. The Baldwin motors proved to be an excellent design, running no fewer than 34 681 kilometres in service in their first five months. Although the eight cars were 'very light and subjected repeatedly to more than twice the load they were constructed to carry, they have stood the strain remarkably well'.[3] Furthermore, as Charles Goodchap, commissioner of railways, reported, they had returned a profit representing a third of the capital investment over a year.

It was no wonder that the omnibus proprietors were angry as they saw their business destroyed. John Young tried once more to obtain permission for a system of private horse tramways, but he tried in vain. His was the true voice of private enterprise when he complained that, 'I never heard of Government working tramways, neither in New Zealand or South Australia nor elsewhere'.[4] One of his supporters, Edward Combes, stated: 'I am not at all favourable to the present motor; I never saw a worse; and I think that the carriages themselves the greatest possible abortions . . . I think, that the work of that line could be as well done by horses as by steam'.[5]

The plain fact was that the government had made a success of their tramways, the city needed them, and the people wanted them extended. The temporary tramway became permanent. By the time four years had passed there were over 40 kilometres of tramways in Sydney, 58 steam motors were in service and almost 26 million fares were being collected annually. As each new suburban line was added, congestion at the city terminal became severe, with the trams queued up as each motor shunted its trailers. This was helped a little by an extension to an off-street yard at Bridge Street, but the steam trams were always plagued by the constraint of their entry to the city by only a single street. No progress was made against the prejudice of

Tram near Sydney University. *(Mitchell Library)*

'One of the worst punishments that a man can undergo'; catching the bus on a rainy night, 1879. *(Australasian Sketcher)*

Double deck tram in George Street West, now called Broadway. *(National Library)*

Tram in Elizabeth Street. *(Mitchell Library)*

local interests in other streets until the coming of the electric trams.

In other parts of the world, steam trams did not find great favour in city operation. British motors, burdened with local anti-pollution regulations, tended to be underpowered and uninspiring. Always they were blamed for their noise and grime. Sydney was probably the first large-scale application of steam power to a tramway and it was only surpassed in size by the steam tramways of Paris. Sydney was also a pioneer in government ownership of its tramways from the outset.

The little tram motors proved their worth on some quite taxing hills in the eastern suburbs. The pull up from Coogee beach was a special trial, but the motor and its two trailers would slowly breast the 1 in 20 grade, the white plume of steam standing out against the green grass of the Pacific slopes, while a full crowd of happy picnickers and sandy children would think of home and dinner waiting.

With their popularity, the trams were often grossly overcrowded, which led the railway commissioner to issue a notice in 1881 to the effect that single-decked cars were designed for 60 passengers and double-decked cars for 90. Because the cars had been damaged by overcrowding, it was announced that the conductors had orders to prevent excessive numbers from getting aboard. It was probably a rule obeyed in the breach. G.V. Portus recalled:

> At peak periods during the day and for cricket matches and race meetings, huge double-decker cars were used. Dirty and noisy as they were, I have never seen a tram service that could shift a crowd more quickly. A few five-car trams with their puffing locomotives could cut a Sydney Cricket Ground crowd down to half in no time.[6]

If you were a person of substance, you might well find that the tramway workers were larrikins, as Mr O'Connor, the MP for West Sydney, found in 1882. He noted that 'The drivers of the motors held a terrible power of destruction in their hands'. He had been driving up King Street, and had just been given the signal to cross.

> Just as he got over the first rail a motor came up at a tremendous pace, and passed the spot at which it was supposed to stop. Had he been an old man, or nervous, or had he lost his presence of mind, he would have been ground into a thousand pieces. He had an active horse, and directly that he saw that the motor was rushing towards the buggy he turned the horse round and ran down the line, and thus saved himself.[7]

When O'Connor went to the tramway office to complain, 'the officers there began to laugh and jeer at him; but the supervisor was not there'.

The puffing of the tram and its shrill whistle at the street corners was becoming commonplace, and the slow spread of the main Sydney network was

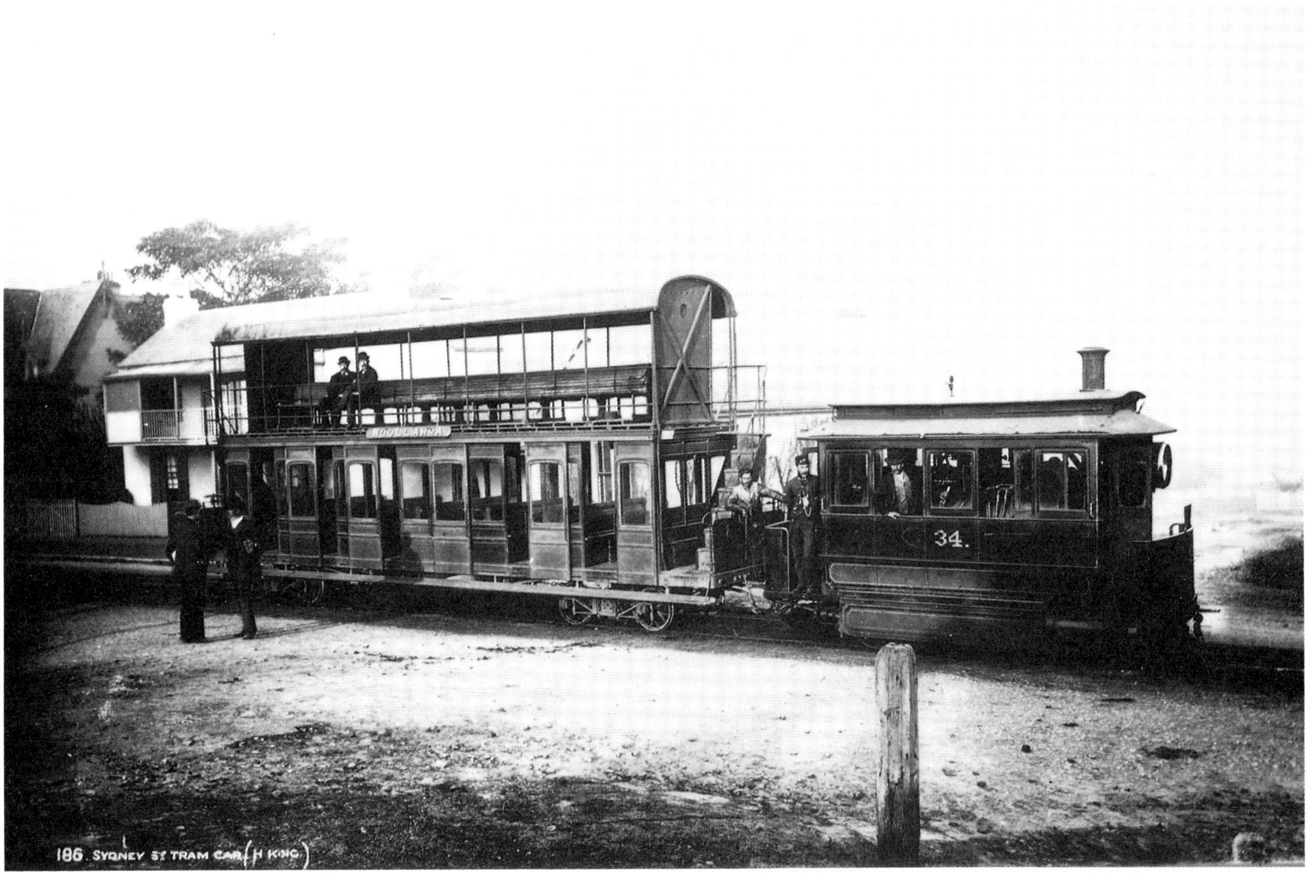

Double-deck tram for Woollahra. *(National Library)*

Newcastle tram, bound for Broadmeadow, pauses for a military procession. *(National Library)*

Tramcar and its builders. *(Mitchell Library)*

matched by developments in other areas. The first of these was at Parramatta, the third-largest town in the colony. From the earliest times, Parramatta had been linked to Sydney by water and the steam ferries provided the most comfortable journey between the two until the coming of the railway. By the end of the 1870s, a gentleman named Charles Jeanneret had taken over the Parramatta ferry services, only to find that the silting of the Parramatta River was preventing his steamers reaching the town quay with any reliability. In October 1883 he opened his own steam tramway from central Parramatta to Queens Wharf, four kilometres down the river, where the navigation was assured and from where the *Alathea* or one of the other ferries could take passengers on to Sydney or one of the harbourside suburbs.

The second private tramway belonged to a man named Thomas Saywell. When the railway was opened to Hurstville in 1884 it passed 2.5 kilometres west of his real estate interests by the shores of Botany Bay. To aid development, he built a steam tramway from the railway at Rockdale and opened it with hired Railway Department equipment on the Prince of Wales' birthday holiday in November 1885. As attractions for people to come to Botany Bay he offered, at the end of his tramway, the Brighton Hotel, the Shady Nook picnic grounds, a shark-proof bathing enclosure and a racecourse.

Newcastle, the second city of the colony, saw its first steam trams in July 1887 when the government system opened. For Newcastle, the Cinderella city, second-best was always good enough in the eyes of the Railway Department. There had been experiments in Sydney with self-contained steam trams, where the boiler and machinery were in the car instead of in a separate locomotive. These had been a great disappointment in service but as Newcastle was a flatter place they were considered to be more suitable there, though with their top decks cut off because of the low bridges. In Sydney they had been known as 'jumbos' and the name remained in Newcastle, as did their poor reputation. On the occasion of what was to have been an official opening of the service, the mayor of Newcastle, in his ermine and chain of office, rode out on the tram to the faithful cheers of his constituents. The tram derailed on Lambton Hill at some faulty points and fell off the track, so the Mayor, 'who went out resplendent in his robes had to be brought back in a cart like a coster monger'.[8]

When services were commenced they were still plagued with problems, as one old resident recalled:

> A tram loaded with passengers for Newcastle, who were having an unpleasant journey on account of frequent stoppages, were amused when the 'Jumbo' refused duty altogether, and the driver . . . stepped from his tram and went to a shop down the street. He returned with a piece of string which he tied somewhere and we continued the journey without further trouble.[9]

These white elephants were soon displaced by the reliable Baldwin tram motors.

Through the 1880s, as the Sydney tramways expanded, they became indispensable to the life of the city. Between 1883 and 1888 patronage doubled, and it was to grow steadily until 1893, when the depression intervened. The tram motors worked very hard, each running an average of 40 000 kilometres a year — more, even, than the average of the department's main-line railway locomotives. Some motors would run as many as 55 000 kilometres in a year. Unlike the railway locomotives, the tram motors were in daily contact with the dusty streets; they were constantly stopping and starting with heavy loads; and as a result they required a substantial effort at maintenance. This was supplied by a large staff at the Randwick workshops at night, on penalty rates. The whole operation was expensive, but worthwhile. Like the motors, the tramway men worked long hours.

Typical, probably, was Richard Walker, whose diary provides a detailed description of his work during 1887 and 1888. At this time a driver earned 13 *s.* a day. Before his permanent promotion to the rank of steam driver, Richard Walker worked the night shifts, starting at 9 p.m. and working through to as late as 8.30 next morning. During this time he might be shunting, or hauling another motor to Randwick for repair, or he might just be on shed duty. Later, as a permanent driver, he would be hauling trams in the streets all day from 7.30 a.m. to 12.30 p.m., and from 3.00 to 7.20 p.m. While a working day of somewhat over nine hours was usual, he might work as long as 13 hours at a stretch, driving his motor backwards and forwards through the Sydney streets. A typical day's work would see him at Pitt Street with fireman Patrick Bourke aboard engine number 81; at 8.00 a.m. nosing out into the street with cars 50 and 123 (one single-deck and one double-deck) in tow. The first run would be out to Enmore and back to Bridge Street, then to Glebe Point and back. The morning would end by taking five cars out to Moore Park and then returning the motor to the depot. The afternoon would start by going to Moore Park to bring back four cars, then entering the peak-hour traffic with cars 48 and 87, both double-deckers, for return trips to Newtown Bridge and Enmore. With the home-going crowds, the trip to Newtown took 35 minutes, but returning almost empty to the city took five minutes less. As he signed off for the day, Richard Walker noted that engine 81 had used 10 bags of coke, three pots of oil, one can of tallow and .3 kilos of cotton waste. On a long Saturday afternoon he might take two double-decked cars out to Coogee Bay for four return trips, 43 minutes each way. In 1893, after 11 years on the trams, Richard Walker was obliged to resign from his position, as his superiors considered that his activities in land speculation were incompatible with his position as a public servant![10]

The conductors on the trams were another race altogether. As all cars were of the crossbench configuration which became known as a 'toastrack', the conductor was, more often than not, clinging to the side of the tram on the footboard, collecting fares, rain or shine, as the tram charged along with a host of horse-drawn vehicles perhaps only a hair's-breadth away. As the years went on, the cars were considered not strong enough to support their top decks any longer and were cut down. The conductor, sure of hand and foot, would be working on the footboard

Tram for Paddington near Hyde Park. *(LaTrobe Library)*

Tram by the Great Synagogue in Elizabeth Street. The building and the tram are close contemporaries. *(Mitchell Library)*

right into an era of mechanised transport, for almost as long as the trams lasted. The newsboys also were an agile race, as they sold their newspapers along the footboards, even crossing from tram to tram without touching the ground. Despite the extent to which the Sydney tramways grew, and the size of the depots that served them, the staff and their individual idiosyncrasies were often very well known to the public; those who were cheery, those who were not, those who could be relied upon for a tip on the races, and so on.

Crossbench cars suited Sydney. They were airy in summer and the huge crowds they could carry were disgorged at Randwick Racecourse or some other place of popular pilgrimage almost in an instant.

It was of the Sydney of the steam trams that Banjo Paterson wrote in his 'Clancy of the Overflow'.

And in place of lowing cattle, I can hear the fiendish rattle
Of the tramways and the buses making hurry down the street;
And the language uninviting of the gutter children fighting
Comes fitfully and faintly through the ceaseless tramp of feet.[11]

4

Cable Car

In the cool first light of a summer morning in 1873, seven men stood at the top of a hill in San Francisco with a sense of awe and expectancy. They were out before the rest of the city for fear that they would witness a failure, because two of their number, Andrew Hallidie and William Eppelsheimer, had invented something new in the world. Hallidie spun a screw wheel and the vehicle on which the men stood, gripping onto a cable moving under the street, glided easily and safely down the steep slope towards San Francisco Bay. The cable tram had been born.

In a city that depended on the horse or the steam locomotive, San Francisco's hills were a formidable obstacle. But the inventive mind of Andrew Hallidie turned to the application of the wire rope that his company manufactured to the problem. Mines already used aerial ropeways to carry buckets, and the idea grew on Hallidie that the same technology could be used to haul a tramcar. With the help of Eppelsheimer he devised a scheme whereby an endless rope would run in a tunnel under the street, hauled by a stationary steam engine. The tramcar would be provided with a gripping mechanism which could grasp the rope through a slot in the road surface, and by which the tram could be connected to or disconnected from the rope at will. The rope would thus haul the tram, without the necessity for horses or steam locomotives, for a considerable distance, and up gradients impossible to other forms of transport. Unlike a funicular, in which the cars are permanently attached to the cable, the grip mechanism would allow a large number of trams on the one route, all stopping and starting as necessary. The strains imposed on the cable were accommodated by a complex series of wheels, counter weights and tensioning devices in the engine house.

A cable tramway was expensive to build. The slot had to be kept true in the street by steel yokes set in concrete and the tunnel was lined with pulleys and other gear to make sure that the cable ran properly. But once it was operating it had significant advantages over a horsecar line, in speed, cheapness, frequency of service, and an absence of pollution. The cable car went up hills as fast as it went down, in apparent defiance of gravity, and its quietness made it seem like a ride on a magic carpet. The only difficulty was in going around corners. The rope could go around a corner on a big wheel under the street, but the gripman would have to let go at this point or have the gripper damaged. It was not until 1878 that any cable car was able to go round a corner, and that was by letting go of the rope and coasting around until the next rope could be picked up. This was satisfactory on relatively flat ground, but it could not be done with a curve on a steep hill.

Turning the car in San Francisco. The slot is clearly shown. *(C. Jones)*

The solution of the problem was left to a young New Zealand engineer of Scots descent, George Duncan. When considering the design of the first cable tramway outside San Francisco — that in Dunedin — George Duncan hit on the idea while watching his wife sewing. By the use of all her cotton reels he was able to demonstrate how he would use a number of drum pulleys to take a cable around a curve with the tram still gripping it. The first pull-curve on a cable tramway in the world went into use in 1881 outside St Joseph's Cathedral in Dunedin. Duncan built the Dunedin cable tramways, which included the world's steepest, with a gradient of an incredible 1 in 3.5, and he was responsible for the very fine system that was built in Melbourne.

Among the Australian cities, Melbourne was unique in having a well-developed network of suburban railways by the 1860s, and therefore it was not entirely surprising that it did not see its first horse omnibus until 1869. The omnibus company was the brainchild of Francis Clapp, an American who had come to Victoria in 1853 in the great influx of the gold rush era. Like his contemporary, George Train, he was a man of great energy, developing coaching lines and importing the latest American-designed buggies and other vehicles. In 1860 he was negotiating to build a horse tramway in Melbourne, but the project lapsed. From 1869 onwards, however, every route that Clapp's company ran, and every building that it bought, was with an eye to the eventual conversion of the omnibus system to a tramway.

Another attempt to gain the necessary legislative authority failed in 1872, but with hopes still high, Clapp had his company liquidated in 1877 and reconstituted as the Melbourne Tramway & Omnibus Company. In 1882 a bill to authorise the tramways that he had for so long desired entered the Victorian parliament. There was opposition from those who branded the company's proposals as enshrining a monopoly, and from those who feared that the noise and danger of Sydney's steam trams would be imported to the southern metropolis. In the usual manner in which these things were done, consideration of the legislation went to public hearings by a select committee of the parliament. It was only at this stage that it was revealed that the company intended its proposed 70 kilometres of tramway to be worked in some parts by horses, and in others by the new 'wire cable system' now proving so successful in San Francisco, Dunedin and Chicago.[1]

It was made plain that the cost of stabling, feeding and grooming each of the company's 1700 omnibus horses each year was £100, and that cable would provide a saving of more than 35 per cent of the operating costs of a horse tramway. Support also came from private individuals. William Buckhurst, an estate agent of Emerald Hill, pointed out how much the omnibuses had developed his suburb. He drew an analogy of technological progress from the way paddle steamers had been replaced by screw steamers and applied it to tramways: 'All I know is that everywhere there is steam power (the most monstrous case of all is Sydney) it is becoming unpopular and dropping into disuse, and horse power is superseding it, and wherever practicable, the endless chain will supersede horse power'. He finished his evidence on a very positive note:

> My experience in Adelaide, San Francisco, and other places, is, that after people have once tried tramways, they would as soon think of doing away with them as with the butcher or the baker; they become a necessity, and the only surprise here, after we have adopted them, will be that we had not done so years ago.[2]

The canny Clapp, who had never yet run an omnibus line that made a loss, was now thinking more and more of applying full scale cable traction to his proposed tramways. The committee was evidently impressed that even the mother city of London, which had stood out firmly against the building of horse tramways within the boundaries of the city, was considering two cable lines.

Francis Clapp's initiatives might almost have gone the way of those of John Young in Sydney, as a change in government early in 1883 might well have seen the proposed legislation lapse had not Duncan Gillies, the original sponsor of the Bill, and now minister for railways, given it his active support. The Melbourne Tramway & Omnibus Company's Act was finally passed in the spring of 1883.

The Melbourne tramlines were to be built by a Tramway Trust with powers to borrow money for the work, and which would lease them to the company until 1916. The company would pay interest on the loan and contribute to a sinking fund. Francis Clapp, now firmly allied with George Duncan, determined that Melbourne would have cable trams, that it would very probably be the largest system of its kind in the world, and that it would certainly be the best.

The first route was to run from Spencer Street Station to Hawthorn Bridge via Flinders Street, Wellington Parade and Bridge Road. The excavations began in October 1884 and the work was to go on for seven years until the whole 74 kilometres of cable tramway were complete. The disruption was considerable, but so was the work which had to be done. Between the tracks, tunnels were dug to carry the cable. They were 1.14 metres deep, concrete lined and reinforced by thousands upon thousands of steel yokes, bent to a horseshoe shape, which carried the slot beams. These appeared on the surface of the street like a third track. Every ten metres there was a manhole for inspection, and under it a 23 centimetre pulley, mounted so as to support the weight of the cable. With the extra gear required on corners and in the engine house, a cable tramway absorbed enough steel to build three times the length of ordinary railway.

Each line had its engine house, a simple but classically-styled brick building, dominated by a tall chimney. The engine house for the Richmond line,

Trams by Parliament. *(postcard)*

Trams in Collins Street. *(C. Jones collection)*

Tram at St Kilda Junction. *(C. Jones collection)*

situated on the corner of Bridge and Punt Roads, issued two ropes, one towards the city and one towards Richmond. The standard rope had a circumference of 89 millimetres and consisted of six strands of seven wires on a hemp core, with a weight of 3.9 kilograms per metre. An average length of rope would weigh over 25 tonnes. In Collins Street and St Kilda Road, where there was heavier traffic, the ropes used were of greater thickness and strength. Thus, quite an amount of the energy generated in each engine house was used just to haul the cables around, without the weight of the trams and their passengers.

It was quite an experience to see the first cables unloaded from the ship in the Yarra, coiled onto waggons and taken through the streets to the engine house. By the latter part of October 1885, after a year's work, it was time to lay the first cable. Early in the morning a team of ten strong horses was hitched to one of the gripper cars to which the end of the cable was attached. As it ran out into the tunnel it was liberally doused with oil to keep it running smoothly. Along the way, relays of men were ready to signal with flags that all was going as it should. At Hawthorn Bridge the cable was led around the two big wheels to the return track, six more horses were added to the team and the rope was led back again to the engine house and spliced into an endless loop. As, in the course of time, each cable needed to be replaced, the new rope would be drawn into its place by the old, with no sign from the street that anything unusual was happening.

The Argus noted the complete success of the Richmond line during the period when tests were being run and drivers trained: 'In the streets the only noise heard was a slight humming from the cable as it runs on its bearings. In the engine house the tension gear and other automatic arrangements all worked well, and the massive engines and driving wheels went smoothly.'[3]

In fact the whole operation of the new system was introduced smoothly. At the end of October 1885 the members of the Tramway Trust rode the length of the Richmond line to mark its completion, and on 11 November full passenger service commenced.[4] Twenty tram sets were ready for service, all from the well-known workshop of John Stephenson of New York.

The Melbourne cable trams followed the classical American pattern, and in the course of their life the design was changed almost not at all. In front was the grip car, known as the 'dummy'. This name originated in America where it applied to steam tram motors, which carried no passengers but were made to look like tramcars, and so were dummy trams. The name was used for the early San Francisco grip cars and it stuck, although the Melbourne dummies could seat

Tram posed in Lonsdale Street. *(Mitchell Library)*

Big Brunswick car. *(MMTB)*

Fitzroy Street at St Kilda Junction. Another photographer has stopped the tram and looks into his viewfinder. Luckily the motor traffic is light. *(postcard)*

20 people and carry as many more as could grip onto something solid while they stood around the edge. In the middle stood the gripman, or 'grippie' as he was more usually known, to control the tram through the big levers that closed or opened the jaws of the gripper on the cable, or apply the brakes. Above his head was the bell which he had to ring frequently to advertise the presence of the tram to any cross traffic. When the tram was stopped the cable ran freely through the gripper; then, when the gripman pulled on the lever it would engage the cable and the tram would slide effortlessly forward. The cable trams were amazingly quiet, gliding like a swan, as some people commented. Behind the dummy was the car, with 22 seats inside. At each terminus it had to be shunted around to the other end of the dummy, either by gravity or by fly shunting — in the latter process the car would be detached while the tramset was still in motion. The dummy would pull clear and cross over to the other track and the car would be allowed to run past it and cross over further down. The two would then be joined up again ready for the return journey. The whole business became quite an art, requiring speed and split-second timing, at which the tram crews were adept. In the peak hour at the foot of Elizabeth Street, opposite Flinders Street Station, 176 trams would shunt at the rate of one every 20 seconds.

For the heavier traffic from Elizabeth Street to Brunswick, larger cars were built so that a single tramset could carry 122 passengers, a similar number to a modern electric tram. For periods of heavier traffic, more cars could be added, and this was frequently done in America, but the biggest cable cars ever built were used in Edinburgh, in Scotland. These cumbersome double-deckers had a double-sided gripper at both ends so they could handle the numerous auxiliary cables that they required to get them around corners.

In Melbourne, the trams usually let go the rope and went around under momentum. At St Kilda Junction there was a long curve where a tram, meeting a strong headwind in the winter, might actually not make it as far as the next rope. The passengers would then get out and push. Thomas Wood, in 1930, regretted that he never saw it happen.

The initial speed of the Melbourne cables was only 9.7 kilometres per hour, so the trams would match the speed of the buses and not frighten the horses, especially where the traffic was heavy, as in Flinders and Swanston Streets. It was soon found that the cables could be run faster and the speeds gradually increased over the years so that, in the 1920s, 15 ropes were running at more than 21 kilometres per hour and the other 11 at over 18 kilometres per hour. Melbourne

Opening day, Richmond, 1885. *(C. Jones collection)*

Chapel Street, 1903. *(The Australasian)*

therefore became one of the world's fastest cable tramways, though none of the ropes ever ran at the Chicago speed of a record 23.7 kilometres per hour. In San Francisco today the ropes are run at a modest 14.5 kilometres per hour.

Before the final speeding up of the system it was noted that the average speed with stops was 14.5 kilometres per hour, actually a little faster than the average speed achieved in service by the Sydney electric trams.

This was how they seemed to one young man of the time:

> When he received the signal to start from the conductor, the gripman went bong! bong! on his bell, released the brake lever, and pulled back slowly on the grip. The passengers felt first a slight shudder as the car nudged forward, rather as of an automobile with an imperfect clutch; next a sudden and exhilarating jerk as the claw clamped firmly onto the cable and the little equipage was drawn smoothly forward with no sound except for the soft swish of the wheels.[5]

As with the Adelaide horse trams, it was not expected that gentlemen would wait for the tram to stop completely before getting on or off, though ladies were a different case. It was always possible to run for the tram and leap aboard, gripping one of the roof staunchions of the dummy, and likewise a reasonable agility would see a man safely off again if he wished. One of Frank Hardy's characters in *Power Without Glory* paid the price of trying to do it while too full of post-electoral good spirits: ' "Jees, I've gorn past me stop!" Sugar exclaimed. He swayed for a moment holding the upright rail of the tram, then leapt off to be hurtled through the air and roll in an undignified ball in the gutter.'[6] A smart boy might avoid paying his fare by a certain nimbleness around the outside of the tram in avoiding the conductor.

Toorak engine house. *(LaTrobe Library)*

In the days when the Scots, rather than the Irish, were the regular butt of jokes, a story was told of a young Scotsman who boarded a cable tram and asked the fare to the city. The conductor told him it was twopence. At this the Scotsman jumped off the tram and proceeded to run along behind. After going about a mile like this he shouted out to the conductor to ask

Tram to the football, 1908. *(The Australasian)*

Tram in Bourke Street, 1937. *(M. Jones)*

Flinders Street Station, 1925; city workers head for home at lunchtime on Saturday. *(Vicrail)*

Busy urban scene in King William Street. All kinds of vehicles mix together, from the trams and cabs to a rich man's carriage. Parked discreetly is a lone motor car. *(postcard)*

West Melbourne car by Law Courts. *(postcard)*

Author's wife rings the bell on the dummy. *(C. Jones)*

North Carlton and St Kilda car. *(C. Jones)*

Queen Street, Brisbane. *(postcard)*

J-class tram and St Mary's. *(postcard)*

L-class tram and crowds in Pitt Street. The California Combination design was to prove inadequate for the Sydney crowds, and these trams were eventually converted to full crossbench style. *(postcard)*

Trams in King William Street. The pride and relief of the people of Adelaide at their new tramways were illustrated by many different postcards. *(postcard)*

Trams at Circular Quay. An E-class set is leaving for Bondi. *(postcard)*

what the fare was now. 'It's threepence,' said the conductor. 'The city is in the other direction!'[7]

The other thing that could be done with the cable by young boys was to try to ensnare it with some string with a tin can on the end. When this was done, the tin can would noisily bounce off up the road, apparently with a mind of its own, and the boys could amuse themselves by trying to hit it with stones, to the fury of the authorities. The children of these same boys would later be looking for an electric tram to flatten a penny on the track with its wheels.

The second line to be built was from Collins Street to North Fitzroy, a busy route that required 40 tramsets. This line, and its branch to Victoria Bridge, opened in 1886. Four more lines opened in 1887 and by 1891 the whole system was complete. By this time, as some of the less profitable lines in San Francisco had already closed, the Melbourne system was the largest cable tramway in the world, and it was to retain that position until the early 1930s. In its layout and construction, thanks to George Duncan, it was always the best, without the excesses of over-long ropes or undue curvature that caused the early closure of several American systems. Its very longevity indicates its quality.

A story is told of San Francisco that a Chinese, seeing the cable cars stranded motionless all along the street, asked, 'What's a matter, stling bloke?' In fact, a break in the cable was extremely rare, but this did not prevent the cable being the most troublesome part of the whole system. A cable would last only about six months before it had to be replaced. In the meantime the constant twisting and straightening as it went on its way introduced wear and possible stranding. A loose strand could damage the equipment, or become tangled in a gripper. Melbourne managed to avoid an accident of the kind that was visited upon San Francisco in 1971 when a frayed cable became entangled in a gripper and five cable cars had smashed together helplessly before the rope was stopped. A stranded cable had to be mended promptly, and meanwhile all the cars on the line had to sit and wait. This could take some hours, though the record repair in Melbourne was accomplished in 23 minutes. Where the cables crossed, one would have to go below the other and the tram on this line would have to let go of the rope at the crossing. It was the convention that the senior cable — that is, the one laid first — would be on top. In both Elizabeth and Swanston Streets, the cable was the junior and all the trams starting from a stop would have to accelerate as quickly as they could towards the street corner, then drop the cable and coast across to pick it up on the other side. The gripman of the tram from St Kilda Beach to North Carlton would have eight rope drops, either for changing cables or for avoiding cross ropes.[8] Usually the mechanism

Collins Street. *(stereograph)*

Car and Tram by Flinders Street Station. *(Herald and Weekly Times)*

under the street ensured that the new cable was fed automatically into the jaws of the gripper. If the gripman forgot to throw the cable when it was required it would be pulled out by another mechanism, though not without some damage to the gripper. It was a cardinal rule that it was better to damage the gripper than the cable.

One story, which today might stretch credulity a little, was told of Abdul Guest, a gripman well-known to passengers, who had previously been a conductor and who wore a chestfull of medal ribbons. It is said that one Carlton hotel would always have a beer set up for him when his tram was due. As the tram approached the corner he would throw the rope and, with a cry of 'Mind the curve', leap off, run into the pub, down his beer, then run out the other side to join the tram, which by then had coasted into the next street. Such characters have not entirely vanished, as

Mornington cable car, Dunedin. *(Alexander Turnbull Library)*

some people will vividly recall one particular conductor blowing bubbles out of the door of the tram all the way up St Kilda Road.

In a mechanical age the cable trams were a mechanical marvel. The people of Melbourne quickly took them to their hearts, and even in Sydney the authorities were not unaware that here was a solution to one of their problems.

After the establishment in 1878 of a permanent North Shore ferry service, Sydney's suburban expansion began to extend up the steep harbour slopes of North Sydney. Pressure for the introduction of a tram service to connect with the ferry and save people the strenuous walk uphill was met with the admission that this was beyond the capabilities of steam trams. However, developments in Melbourne were watched with great interest, and George Duncan himself was called in to design a cable tramway from the wharf at Milsons Point to the top of Ridge Street. The line, which opened in 1886, was initially equipped with eight tramsets similar to, but smaller than, the ones in Melbourne. The trams met all the ferries and at peak hours, when a boat such as the *Cammeray* might be carrying over 600 people, several trams would be needed at the one time. In these circumstances the first tram would run express to Walker Street and the following tram would stop wherever it was required. The line was later extended to Crows Nest. The second cable line in Sydney was built on King Street to carry traffic from the ferries at Erskine Street into the city and out via Queens Cross (as Kings Cross was then known) to Edgecliff. It was opened in 1894, but for Sydney, a latecomer to the acceptance of cable technology, there were to be no further cable lines. The winds of change were blowing through the tramways of the world and they were bringing with them a virtual revolution in urban life, the electric tram.

5

An Electric Spark

In 1888 Australia celebrated the centenary of its first white settlement. At the peak of a high tide of colonial confidence, Victoria crowned the event with a grand international Centennial Exhibition, an exhibition Sydney was prevented from rivalling since the burning of the Garden Palace in 1882. All of the progress of the colonies and all their art and culture stood side by side with the latest productions of the whole civilised world. When the exhibition opened on 1 August, one of the exhibitors was the Thomson-Houston Company of USA, a multinational in the field of electricity. Along with the lamps, motors and transformers, was a mobile exhibit that ran along the northern boundary of the exhibition grounds, Australia's first electric tram.

The idea of the electric tram had been around for some time, but the early versions suffered from several defects which rendered them unsuitable for the work of cities. Ernst Siemens' first tram in 1881 had gathered its current from the running rails and Leo Daft used a similar system four years later in Baltimore. The danger of live rails in the road was obvious, but the solution to the problem took a while to reach. Trials were made of a system whereby current was gathered from a live overhead wire by means of a little trolley that ran along it, towed by a wire from the tram it powered. The little trolley could be a bit unstable and passengers were understandably upset when it left its wires and crashed down on the roof. The transmission of power from the motor to the wheels was another problem that proved difficult to solve. By 1887 the device of a trolley pole with a wheel on its end, held against the underside of the wire by a spring at its base, had been realised and in that year a former naval officer, Frank Sprague, supplied a whole new system of tramways to the city of Richmond, Virginia. This pioneer system had not overcome its teething troubles and entered revenue operation until January 1888, but it was sufficiently impressive for the citizens of Boston to scrap any idea of converting their horse tramways to cable, and to turn to electricity. The idea of the trolley car was to sweep America, and in 1888 Melbourne looked as though it would be with them.

When the Centennial Exhibition closed in March 1889 the tram and its equipment were sold to the Box Hill & Doncaster Tramway Co. Ltd, which intended to run it from the railway at Box Hill to the Doncaster Tower, where it would attract sightseers both to the tower's magnificent views and to the blandishments of the associated hotel, in the hope that the land of the Doncaster area would be opened up for subdivision at a good profit. When the line was opened on 14 October 1889 it ran for most of its 3.6 kilometres through open pastoral country. *The Age*, with an uncertain grasp on the technology involved in the electrical system, commented, 'It is thought that this system will prove more feasible than the method of driving cars from electricity stored in jars, but at present the matter has scarcely emerged from the experimental stage'.[1]

Initially, the popularity of the service was such that a second tram had to be added, but the line was soon to run into more than its fair share of troubles. The landowners through whose properties the road for the tramway had been built felt that they had been inadequately compensated, and in mid-1891 onc gentleman went so far as to build his fences back across

J-class trams at Queens Square, Sydney. *(postcard)*

F-class trams at Circular Quay, 1903. The ferry *Courier* is at the Watsons Bay jetty, and the steamer *Sierra* in the background will be sailing for Vancouver. *(G. Andrews collection)*

the tramline. The tramway company tore them down, after which the landowner chopped down the tramway poles, thus bringing the service to an abrupt halt. Incensed residents of Doncaster then burnt the landowner in question in effigy, hanging from the tram wires outside the Tower Hotel.

A new start was made early in 1892 by a new company, and with a route carefully amended to avoid the contentious land. Henry Hilton was appointed engineer, and it was to be his herculean struggle which kept the tramway running as long as it did. By 1894, in the general atmosphere of economic disaster, with the banks closing their doors and investments in land rendered worthless, the company was at the end of the road. As a last attempt to recoup some of its investment, it leased the line to Henry Hilton for 1 *s.* a week. Optimism and hard work were not enough, the times being what they were, and the pioneer electric tramway closed for the last time in the first week of 1896.

One of Henry Hilton's memories of the line deserves recall. On one occasion a special excursion was booked for a religious revival meeting at Doncaster. The party coming from Box Hill numbered 45, which was rather more than the total capacity of the tram, but they managed to squeeze aboard. It was the custom for the trolley pole to be tied down as the tram left Doncaster and for the descent to Koonung Creek to be made under gravity. When the overloaded tram left at 10 p.m., someone, siezed with the spirit of the occasion, started up the hymn beginning with the words 'Ho, my comrades! See the signal'. At the same time the driver was discovering, to his horror, that the brake was having no effect and the tram could only plummet downhill out of control. 'Hold the fort, for I am coming!' roared the passengers in chorus, all oblivious to their real danger. At the bottom, by virtue either of good engineering or divine intervention, the

Trams at Circular Quay. *(G. Andrews collection)*

Tram at Darling Street Wharf. The counterweight, which prevented cars running away on the 1 in 8.24 grade, is seen behind. *(National Library)*

tram took the awkward curve on the bridge without faltering and sailed away up the line through the dark fields towards Box Hill.[2]

In Sydney the new technology was under consideration at the same time. The idea was that all of the new electrical systems, including battery trams, should be given a trial to ascertain which was best and which could provide a cheap and efficient alternative to the steam trams. Had the trial been undertaken earlier, the King Street cable tramway might never have been built. As in Melbourne, it was the Thomson-Houston Company whose electric trams were to be tried. Three saloon trams, attractive in a light varnish and decorated with painted arabesques, were supplied by John Stephenson to run on an electrified section of the steam system between Randwick and Waverley. For 17 months from November 1890 the electric trams were in service, interspersed with steam trams as traffic and breakdowns dictated. The public treated the

Steam and electric trams at the old Redfern Railway Station. *(LaTrobe Library)*

Posing for the opening of a Perth tram line, possibly in 1901. Although it was an English company, American equipment was preferred. *(Library Board of W.A.)*

Tram at Bulimba Ferry. The ferries extended people's journeys beyond the tram terminuses at several points. *(Oxley Library)*

service as a novelty but the tramway authorities were unimpressed, declaring the electric system to be not as economical as they had hoped. The equipment, however, was retained and eventually transferred to North Sydney, where a new line was under construction from the cable tramway at Ridge Street through Cremorne to Spit Junction. As steam trams on the North Shore were likely to be almost the orphaned oddities that the electric trams had been at Waverley, it was decided to try electric traction from the outset. On 20 September 1893, therefore, Sydney's first permanent electric trams nosed their way out of the cable car depot to take their first passengers along Military Road. Services were tentative initially, as the times were depressed and people might not afford the fare, but at peak periods the electric cars would haul cable trailers and soon there was pressure for extensions. After four years the line continued down the hill to Mosman's Bay, where, at the ferry wharf, the cliff was cut back to make the road wide enough for the trams to shunt. The direct ferry service to Circular Quay was a tremendous boost for the tramway. New trams with more powerful motors were built. New extensions were planned. Not only was the North Sydney cable tramway doomed, but the whole of the Sydney steam system could be replaced by electric trams. Sydney was on its way to building one of the largest electric tramways in the world.

In Tasmania, Hobart — late to emerge from its convict economy — was looking towards trams to assist its transition into the modern age. In 1884 the Hobart Tramway Company obtained parliamentary approval to build 13 kilometres of tramway. The gauge chosen, 1067 millimetres, the first narrow-gauge tramway in the colonies, was intended to match that of the island's railways, as it had been envisaged that, as well as passenger traffic, it would also be useful for railway waggons. This industrial use, an old story by this time in places other than Tasmania, was emphasised by the route of the main line, which was to be from the Cascade Brewery to the railway. Because of the grades involved in hilly Hobart, it was proposed that, rather than horse power, steam motors should be used, but the motors would be less offensive than those in Sydney and the cars would be light single-deckers only. The system, with its three branches to Moonah, Cascades and Sandy Bay, was to be the making of the city.

> In the case of Hobart, the attractions of the charming sea beaches at Sandy Bay, and of the picturesque scenery and invigorating air of Mount Wellington (both of which are now practically inaccessible to the working classes and their families) would certainly induce a very large traffic additional on the regular residential traffic, and which would continue throughout the greater part of the year. It is now a very serious evil that residences can only be obtained with great difficulty and at excessive rents, but the conveniences of the tramway would open up a much greater field for selection, and enable cottagers to gratify their usual desire for a piece of garden ground.[3]

For one reason or another, no tramway eventuated. By the end of 1890 the company had managed to lay 2.5 kilometres of track and its promoters were thinking of changing to cable traction in place of steam. This proved a transitory dream, but the patience of the Hobart citizens was rewarded by the evident success of electric tramways in other parts of the world. Horse, steam, cable, all were forgotten as the company contracted with the Siemens company of London to provide all of the equipment for the 13 kilometres of tramway. In 1891, Walter Reichel, chief engineer of Siemens in Germany, had perfected the sliding bow method of current collection from the overhead wires and this was to be applied in Hobart, on double-decked trams of British manufacture. Each of the 20 trams which provided all services in Hobart for the first ten years had two bows. Their supporting frame helped hold the flimsy top cover over the open upper deck.

The Hobart trams commenced the day after those in North Sydney, 21 September 1893. For the first six months, until all the bugs were ironed out, the Siemens company kept control, but then the Hobart Electric Tramway Co. took over. To the eyes of the average mainlander the trams would have seemed very tall, teetering up the hills in the narrow Hobart streets. As in Adelaide, they tended to blossom with advertisements, for the Cascade Brewery Co Ltd, for Wolfe's Schnapps, for Robur Tea 'Grocers Sell It', and so on. Although there would be occasions when the trams were full of happy picnickers in their best summer

Tram at Mount Wellington. The tramline was the gateway to fresh air and nature. *(Tasmanian Library)*

Tram at Toowong. Joseph Badger lived near here for eight years, and steps led up to his backyard. *(postcard)*

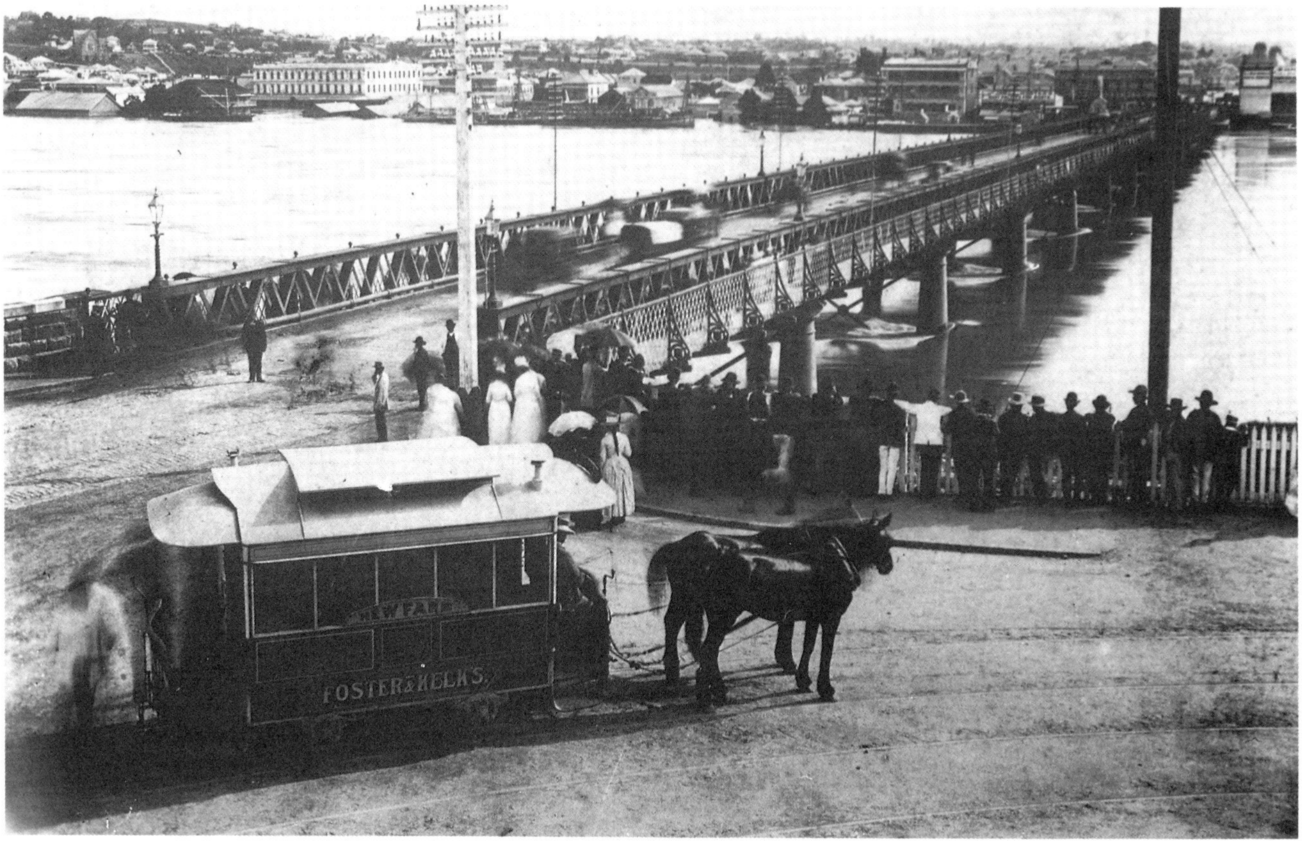

Crowds watch floodwaters at Victoria Bridge while a tram stands in North Quay. The level rose to 6.2 metres in 1890 and 9.2 metres in 1893. *(C. Jones collection)*

clothes and big hats for Sandy Bay, the tramway company never made a big profit. As a result, only small numbers of trams were added to the fleet after 1903 and no extensions of the tracks were undertaken until the system passed under municipal control in 1913. Hobart was unusual among the Australian cities in looking to England rather than to America for its tramway prototypes. It was unique in having the only bogie double-deck electric car to run on an Australian tramway, and the construction of double-deck vehicles did not cease until 1925. The ride on the top deck, with no windows to obstruct the breeze, might be considered quite bracing by mainlanders.

The two other tramways operating in Australia in the early 1890s were in Ballarat and Brisbane. Both used horses and both suffered the usual experience of such undertakings in that they were not particularly profitable.

In Ballarat, the overloading of the cars on the steep pinch in Sturt Street was very hard on the horses, and sometimes they were seen to fall under the strain. By 1891 the police had stated their intention to prevent cruelty to the horses by enforcing load limits on the trams.

It had been the intention of the Queensland Railways to follow the New South Wales example with steam trams, but in the event, a private company opened a horse tramway in 1885. Its nine double deck, nine single deck and two crossbench cars were all built by John Stephenson. During the late 1880s, Brisbane was growing rapidly, but the tramway company found itself unable to make the extensions it needed. The best that could be done to augment services was to provide waggonettes as feeders to and from the several terminuses. What was really needed was electrification. The position was not improved by the situation of the Victoria Bridge. The broad Brisbane River was spanned only twice in its navigable length, by the Victoria Bridge in the city, and the Albert railway bridge at Indooroopilly. The Victoria Bridge had a

Tram in Elizabeth Street, Hobart. *(postcard)*

Second Box Hill tram, 1890, a classical early American design electric tramcar. *(Herald and Weekly Times)*

swing span at its southern end for shipping, and its narrow deck was only wide enough for three vehicles abreast. Consideration was being given to additional bridges, but the problem was solved in 1893.

Cyclonic weather in the first week of February resulted in a veritable deluge in the Brisbane Valley. Two metres of rain fell in five days. The Brisbane River was a roaring destructive torrent, with a recorded height of 7.2 metres above the high tide mark at the Port Office. People gathered at North Quay to watch houses and other debris smashing into the bridge. The last tram crossed on the Saturday, and all day Sunday crowds stood in the rain watching as the water rose and debris piled up. 'As house after house was carried against Victoria Bridge the crash could be heard over everything, and all that was swept onward was smashed to fragments.'[4]

The Albert Bridge, its piers scoured out by the racing water, fell that day. Then at 5.30 a.m. on the Monday morning, with a tremendous heave and roar, the whole northern end of the Victoria Bridge fell, span by span, into the river. Brisbane was cut in half.

In an already depressed situation, when people would walk kilometres in the dark to and from work to save the tram fare, and with all cross-river services temporarily diverted back to the ferry boats, the Metropolitan Tramway and Investment Company was near the end of the line. In 1895 a new company, the Brisbane Tramway Company Limited, was formed to purchase the Brisbane tramways and convert them to electricity. One of its principals was Francis Clapp of Melbourne. New routes were at once surveyed to tap more of the suburban cross-river ferry services and to extend the trams north, south and west, through the valleys and along the ridges of the new suburbs. The technical side of the undertaking was given to the General Electric Company of U.S.A. This company had taken over Thomson-Houston, but its fortunes were at a low ebb in the mid 1890s, and it set out to make Brisbane a showpiece of how an electric tramway should be built. Brisbane thus forged into a temporary lead over Sydney as the first big city in Australia to have a comprehensive electric tramway system.

Responsible for all of this was one of General Electric's best engineers, Joseph Badger. When he came to Brisbane in 1896 he was an energetic New Yorker of age 45. Three years later he was general manager of the company and it was his vision which was to guide the development of the Brisbane tramways for 25 years. Badger was a staunch Presbyterian, who worked with a Bible on his desk. Under his authoritarian paternalistic regime the company flourished. He was not averse to building tramlines where he had no legislative approval, or to having them built specially past the houses where he lived.

When the Brisbane electric tramways opened on 21 June 1897, there were 20 trams, mostly of the

Trams at Mosman Wharf. Each motor tram has to shunt an ex-cable trailer behind the ferry waiting shed. The ferry and tram connection was vital for the development of the North Shore. *(G. Andrews collection)*

'California combination' type, so-called because they followed the layout of the cable cars on California Street in San Francisco. With their open ends and closed centre sections, they became known as 'matchboxes'. To speed the conversion process, Badger had all of the horse trams converted, either to open crossbench cars, or to closed saloons, which in the sweaty climate of Brisbane became known popularly as 'coffins'. In common with the universal experience, the electric tramways wrought a social revolution in Brisbane. Unlike the railways, they followed the settlement closely, helping to consolidate the structure of the city. The value of property would be enhanced by its proximity to the tramline. Some local authorities made substantial financial concessions to ensure that a line came their way. It is no wonder that the trams appear in so many photographs as a symbol of urban pride when it is realised that, in the three years up to 1901, the number of passengers carried almost trebled.

Late in 1899 Perth saw its first electric trams, and at the end of the year they finally penetrated into central Sydney. The event was a spectacular foretaste of things to come as the little trams ran down George Street from the railway to Circular Quay, often so crowded that the drivers had difficulty manipulating their controls for the press of people on the platform. As many as 40 000 people rode the trams during the first day, and although one heedless child was run over and killed at the Quay, it was a great success. As a final gesture, the bus drivers orchestrated a campaign of obstruction of the new electric cars that would soon take away their livelihood. Observers noted that there seemed to be more wool waggons than usual in George Street, and that:

> In one case a man, who was riding a horse and leading two others unattached to a vehicle, deliberately obstructed one of the cars, and when the conductor endeavoured to obtain his name and address the man struck him with a whip. The traffic manager (Mr Kneeshaw) chanced to be on the scene, and immediately gave the man into custody.[5]

Subsequently, trailers were added behind the trams, for the benefit of smokers, and to relieve the crowds.

It was a new era of mobility in Sydney for the average person as the electric web of the tramways spread out into the suburbs. Soon the tramway authorities were having to give serious consideration to the best sort of tram to handle the crowds. It was always common in Sydney for the trams to operate as coupled pairs, and the experience in Britain indicated that the solution might be found in using double-deck trams. In 1907 the theory was given a test, with two of the older trams being given an extra deck and a new design of 80-seat bogie crossbench car being placed in service for comparison. The outcome was never really in doubt. The slow loading and limited standing capacity of the double-deckers told against them. In a city where the inspector at Railway Square had refused to let a pair of motor trams towing a trailer leave for Coogee Beach until all the people got off the roof, the only solution was the fast-loading, high capacity, big crossbench tram. The resulting O class, the ideal tram for the Sydney conditions, came to number 626 units, while the succeeding P class, in the 1920s, numbered a further 258.[6]

6

The Staple of Urban Life

Australians are known as urban dwellers, and as the Victorian era faded with the century and the Edwardian era was born, many people were sharing, in their own way, an urban experience which will never come again. Tramlines were being laid in the gravel roads, electric wires erected, and tram sheds built. People would be watching the progress of the work as the gangs of men dug up the roads to lay the tracks, hoisted the new poles at the roadside, and finally as a tower waggon would come, pulled by a patient horse, from which the copper trolley wire could be fixed in place. Then there would come the great day when, with bunting flying from the shop awnings, a holiday for the school children, all the neighbours out, men, women, children and dogs to see the notables, applaud the speeches and listen to the band, the first electric trams would run. Shining in their new paintwork, maybe a deep chocolate or red lined out in gold, with the tramway company's monogram sandblasted on the glass of the sliding doors to the saloon, the trams were magnificent as they paraded for the first time. The mayor would make a speech in which he would almost certainly compare the previous somnolence of the city or suburb with its present progressive nature, now that the trams had arrived. The tramway manager would make a suitable reply and toasts would be proposed to the King, and to the prosperity of the city and its new form of transport. The day would finish with carnival spirits and free rides for all. 'It makes our suburb appear quite busy,' was the typical comment of a Melbourne resident in 1913.[1]

Apart from virtually sweeping buses from the streets, the trams had several other effects. Where double track was laid, and the trams kept to the left, all the other traffic was obliged to give up the happy chaos of its previous habits and keep to the left also. Thus the trams imposed a proper flow on all street traffic. The introduction of electric trams often came, as it did in Western Australia, at the same time as the introduction of electric power and lighting in people's homes. The trams would help even out the load on the power station, drawing most of their power during the daytime when domestic usage was low, and often

Trams in King William Road. *(postcard)*

Trams, Ballarat. *(postcard)*

raising the usage of an otherwise marginal power utility to more viable proportions. The trams and the electric lights came together in people's minds as a symbol of the progress of a new nation in a new century.

Typically of all electric tramways all over the world, patronage rose in a spectacular manner. As the big Sydney system was built to replace the steam tramways,

Tram and trailer, with a capacity load, Ballarat. *(postcard)*

William Goodman. *(S.A. Archives)*

tram passenger journeys doubled in eight years. In 1911 the equivalent of 345 journeys were made in a year by every man, woman and child in the city. Usage on this level compared closely with the situation in greater New York, where so common were the trams that a baseball team was called the 'Trolley Dodgers', or Dodgers for short. Even in Brisbane, where the number of annual rides per capita in 1911 was 232,

E-class tram set at Circular Quay, waits to depart on the shuttle service to Central Railway Station. *(National Library)*

the situation compared favourably with many of the larger British cities such as Manchester and Liverpool.

The sound of the tram gongs, rung in warning to the unwary, or as a greeting as the cars passed, or to warn of an inspector, were like forest bellbirds in the city streets. The story used to be told of the young lady who was very impressed by the old-world courtesy of one of her young men as he always called her 'fair lady' — until she realised that he worked as a tram conductor.

Everyone, high or low, rode the trams. In Melbourne, politicians such as Stanley Bruce, Edmond Hogan and James Scullin all did so. Australia would be a better place today if present day politicians followed their example. The story is told of how John Wren always rode on the dummy, and always paid his 2 *d.* fare with a florin, which was the only money he ever carried. When he attended a fight at the Stadium he would pay someone to save him a seat on the dummy afterwards. People hanging onto the outside of the car by the window frames could say they could not reach the money in their pockets to pay the fare. They might have their knuckles rapped by the conductor to make them let go. The other lurk was to sit in an open rainy part in the hope that the conductor would be deterred by the weather.

In Western Australia the depression of the 1890s had hardly been felt as the colony basked in the prosperity of its great gold discoveries. New cities arose on the arid plains; Perth experienced a blossoming from what was little more than a sleepy village into a bustling city; and with the changes came the trams. The typical Western Australian tramcar was a big end-loading saloon with a clerestory roof. Built, as many

Rockhampton tram jacked up, 1937. *(Oxley Library)*

Trams in East Street. *(postcard)*

New J-class on the route from the cable terminus at Ocean Street to Rose Bay, 1904. *(National Library)*

THE LATEST ILLUSTRATED SONG—
"Wait for Me" *(Poor Bill).*

"Wait for Me" *(Poor Adelaide).*

The passing of the Adelaide horse trams was none too soon. This postcard, showing a Sydney tram, advertised a contemporary song. *(postcard)*

of them were, in the Philadelphia workshops of J. G. Brill & Co, they would not have looked different from vehicles on a hundred tramways in the United States. Another peculiarly American feature seen in both Perth and Kalgoorlie was the rope-net lifeguard which was hung from the front of the tram to scoop up the unwary pedestrian. In later years, when this was changed for more conventional equipment, hooks were provided on the dashes of the trams from which mothers could hang their prams when they travelled. The sight of the prams waving in the air behind the tram never failed to intrigue visitors from other states.

In Kalgoorlie, the change of shifts at the mines was catered for by the ability of a single tram to tow a whole train of trailers. Something in the order of 280 men could therefore be brought without any difficulty by a single tram from the Boulder Block to central Kalgoorlie. The fortunes of the Kalgoorlie tramways, which came to the city when it had been established only nine years, fluctuated with the mines. But the income of the company was augmented by a positive riot of advertising on the bodies of the trams. A major advertiser, familiar to all Kalgoorlie residents, was J. A. Hicks & Coy Ltd, 'Style Specialists, First with the Latest'. Hicks offered 'Sterling Values' in life-time furniture ('Beautify Your Home with our Modern Furnishings') as well as radio equipment ('All Leading Makes at City Prices'). Hicks' prime position on the side of the tram might be rivalled by other firms' advertisements on the two ends, for instance, Kemp & Jones, whose advertisements included their three addresses and telephone numbers for 'Highest Quality Bacon, Meat and Smallgoods'. Appropriately for a mining town, other advertisers such as Hodgson & Cranston would urge on the public the use of their mining and drilling equipment.

The comprehensive system of tramways in Kalgoorlie and Boulder entered into fierce competition with the suburban railways for passengers and almost managed to run them out of business locally. There were, however, quiet times, when the trams faded under the pitiless sun and the trammies could carry shopping orders for the housewives along the routes.

On a famous occasion in the 1930s, someone hitched the Cafe de Movealong, a mobile cafe that stood in Burt Street in Boulder, by the tram terminus, to the back of a tram by a length of rope. The trammies, who had been having 'one for the road' in the adjacent pub, looked at their watches and made a dash for it, starting the tram with a screeching of wheels and a shower of sparks. Much to the surprise of the patrons, and the outrage of the proprietor, the Cafe de Movealong took off after the tram, hot coals, crockery and pies flying everywhere.[2]

The band plays for the opening of the extension of the Inglewood tram line, in Perth, August 1923. *(W.A. Newspapers)*

Dreadnought tram at Chardon's Hotel, Annerley. The crew pose in their 'foreign legion' caps. *(Oxley Library)*

Boarding the car at the Treasury in Queen Street. Depending on the style of your dress, the high steps could be a trial. *(Oxley Library)*

Tram at Mitcham, an escape to the green hills, 1930. *(S.A. Archives)*

If anyone thought that Kalgoorlie was the end of the line as far as tramways went, there was a surprise in store at the town of Leonora, 225 kilometres to the north. Here, 'progress' had caught up with the dusty mining community on the edge of the desert in the form of a tramline with a single electric tram. It ran for only eight years, until the power station burned down, but during this time it was an amenity which helped maintain the illusion that life at Leonora was almost as civilised as in Perth. The tram was a heavy drain on the limited facilities of the power station. At night, you could tell when the tram was passing by the way the lights dimmed. If it was pulling trailers on the tight bend behind the church at Gwalia the lights might go out altogether. The tram almost met an abrupt end in January 1911 when it ran over four plugs of gelignite, which exploded in rapid succession, though fortunately with insufficient force to do serious damage. *The Argus* reported that: 'Four boys, ranging from eight to nine years of age, have admitted that they placed the gelignite on the rails, and concealed themselves some distance away to see, as one of them said, what it would do to the tram'.[3] What happened to the boys at the hands of authority is not recorded.

All tramway operators made sure that, as well as providing commuter services, they would serve sporting venues and places of natural beauty so people could use the trams for recreation. Tourists would be encouraged to see the sights by tram with elaborate brochures that showed the routes and fares. Fremantle offered a route to parklands at Point Walter, with its panoramic views of the Swan River, spangled with the white sails of the yachts racing. Perth offered a lovely riverside route from the city to Nedlands which was only rivalled in beauty by the long line around the edge of Lake Wendouree in Ballarat. Brisbane also had a riverside line.

The three Victorian provincial cities were, in their own way, ahead of Melbourne in the provision of electric trams. It was basically on the initiative of the local electricity company that the conversion was made from the steam trams in Bendigo and the horse trams in Ballarat. The Electric Supply Company of Victoria Ltd had big plans for Bendigo which were never entirely realised, but they meant that, when the work in Ballarat was commenced there was no longer enough money to build a fancy brick car barn or to provide a fleet of entirely new trams. Luckily, Sydney, which had found that it needed big high-capacity trams, was selling some of its older and smaller ones, and these came to Ballarat second-hand. The old horse trams were retained for use as trailers behind the electric cars for special occasions such as a sporting event or the arrival of a picnic train from Melbourne. The open top decks of the trailers were particularly popular.

Geelong was in festive mood in March 1912 when the Melbourne Electric Supply Co. Ltd commenced the city's first tramways. The streets were filled with holiday crowds and there was much cutting of ribbons and making of speeches as four decorated tramcars paraded through the streets. So it was also in Launceston the previous year. Even old-fashioned conservative Adelaide had taken the plunge.

Adelaide had kept its horse tramways long after they were obsolete. There was no chance, so it seemed, that the private owners would do anything to improve the situation, and so at the end of 1906 the government

Tram at Double Bay, coming down the 1 in 11 grade. *(postcard)*

Tram in Elizabeth Street, Hobart. *(postcard)*

Brisbane Visitor's Guide, c.1908. The tourist was assured, 'Brisbane possesses one of the best electric tramway services in the world'. *(C. Jones collection)*

Tram in Lydiard Street North. The lacy ironwork was also subject to a preservation battle. *(C. Jones)*

Tram in Sturt Street, 1971. *(C. Jones)*

A drop-centre car of the Prahran and Malvern Tramways Trust, beautifully restored to its 1914 condition by the Bendigo Trust. *(C. Jones)*

Sydney O class car in Sydney Museum. *(C. Jones)*

Old trams used for accommodation, Warrumbungle Ranges, 1981. *(C. Jones)*

Perth's last tram, No. 66, waits restoration in 1972. *(C. Jones)*

Tracklaying, Fremantle. *(Fremantle City Council)*

Opening of Launceston tramways, 1911. *(Weekly Courier)*

Two motors and three trailers carry a heavy load from the Kalgoorlie mines, 1931. *(W.A. Government Printer)*

passed legislation to establish the Municipal Tramways Trust. Based to a certain extent on Melbourne, and a model for subsequent organisations in other states, it was empowered to operate electric tramways within 16 kilometres of the GPO. Its board was appointed by the state government, the Adelaide City Council, and a grouping of the suburban councils. The Trust's first act was to buy out all the tramway companies along whose routes it wished to operate. Meanwhile, preparations were in hand for the equipment of the electric system, including a big depot building at Hackney, 100 tramcar bodies from Duncan & Fraser of Franklin Street, and trackwork including a 'grand union' junction at the corner of North Terrace and King William Street. A grand union junction is laid so a tram can proceed in any direction at a cross intersection. Always a rarity, in Australia there were only two, in Adelaide and Melbourne.

From the time that the mayor of Adelaide turned the first sod in May 1908, work went ahead with vigour, removing the old tracks and laying the new, erecting poles and so on. The whole scheme was placed in the hands of William Goodman, chief engineer and general manager of the Trust. Born in England in 1872, he had come to Adelaide with the achievement of the newly constructed electric tramways in Dunedin behind him. He was to remain the guiding hand behind the Adelaide tramways for over 40 years. He ruled the tramways with authority, but also with kindliness, becoming a legend in his own time. As the years went on, the old tramwaymen could tell stories of encounters with the great man; how he had called them by name and promised to consider whatever points they had made to him; or how he had been ruthless in not tolerating sloppy dress or other misdemeanours.

The big day was on 9 March 1909 when Mrs Price, the wife of the premier, 'assisted' William Goodman at the controller of tramcar No.1, which for the occasion was gaily decorated in red, white and blue bunting, as it led a procession of 16 trams with 650 invited guests from Hackney to the city and out to Kensington. The electric trams were a revolution in mobility compared with the horsecars, offering much greater speed and frequency of service. The changeover period was a little confused, as horse and electric trams ran on adjacent tracks, or the horsecars ran on the electric lines themselves, but by 1914 all of the horses had been pensioned off in the city area. Satirical postcards indicated that perhaps it was not before time.

Adelaide was the first in Australia with an innovation often used in America, a 'trolley park'. The Tramways Trust was interested in a property of 79 hectares called Pile's Paddock, which had been intended for subdivision. It arranged for part of the area to be handed over to it for development as a park, while the remainder was sold for building blocks. The value of the land was enhanced by the tramway extension from the Kensington terminus, which opened in 1911, and the tramway was made more attractive by the park at the end, with its rustic bridges, tennis courts, cricket pitches, kiosks and picnic areas. There was an annual sweet pea exhibition. The Tramways Symphonic Band gave regular concerts here, and at Henley Beach. It could also sometimes be seen parading the streets aboard a crossbench tram, in full musical flight. Its conductor, Mr W. H. Foote, was a lecturer at the Elder Conservatorium. When the band was disbanded in 1925 it was only because most people were using their motor cars to come to hear it, rather than the trams. Kensington Gardens were to belong to the tramways for over 20 years.

The only true tramways in tropical Australia were at Rockhampton and Broome. Plans at Townsville failed for lack of capital. The Rockhampton tramways, owned by the city council, opened in time for Carnival Week in June 1909. For the small system which comprised a city belt line and three suburban branches, Rockhampton chose steam power, but uniquely in Australia, the technology was French. The Parisian tramways, which operated self-contained steam trams built by Valentin Purrey at his works in Bordeaux, provided the inspiration for the Queensland venture. The boiler of the tram stood on the front platform with the driver but the firebox door was at floor level and should the driver have to attend to the clinker inside, he would have to stop the tram, get out onto the street and poke it from there. In a city that even Queenslanders admit to be hot, the trams were all of an open crossbench configuration with canvas blinds for wet weather, but the drivers had to be tough as they stood in front of the boiler with the regulator and the brake handle in each hand. While the passengers could choose to sit near to or further from the boiler depending on the weather, the driver was roasted all summer, while in winter he was chilled in front and warmed behind. Such a success was made of the trams that the Railway Department, which ran all its trains through the city down the middle of Denison Street, built two steam railcars of identical design for some of its suburban services. Stopping as they did on every street corner for passengers, they were soon known as the 'tram-trains'.

Rockhampton was provided with cinemas on an almost metropolitan scale. The Earl's Court, Wintergarden and Tivoli together could boast over 5200 seats. It became the practice of the last trams for the night to line up in East Street near the cinemas and for the conductors to call the roll to make sure that all of the shows had finished and that no passengers would be left behind. An occasional humorist would answer for one of the other cinemas to have the trams leave earlier.

After the last trip of the night the drivers tended to race back to the depot at the best speed they could manage. One night the last trams from the Gardens and Dawson Road were racing each other down their two parallel streets, where the routes were only a block apart. At each intersection the drivers could see that the trams were neck and neck, but when the driver of the Gardens tram arrived at the intersection of the two routes he was on his own. The other tram had

Tram in Hay Street, 1933. *(W.A. Government Printer)*

Trams at Kings Cross. *(postcard)*

N-class tram bound for Long Bay, by the Great Synagogue, a nice contrast with the picture on page 24. *(postcard)*

come off the rails on a curve and was sitting in the gutter. Chains and re-railing irons had to be collected from the depot, and it was 3 a.m. before the two chastened drivers could finally put their trams to bed.

Humour could be found even in the misbehaviour of the boilers. During one Carnival Week a heavily loaded tram with two trailers had just gasped in from the Showgrounds to East Street at six kilometres per hour. When the driver asked the driver of the following tram why he had not helped by pushing behind, he replied that he had not been able to catch up. On another occasion a steampipe burst and the driver had to make a hurried exit across the front dash, from where he managed to bring the tram to a halt while standing on the front bumper.

Late in their careers the trams had a big V painted on their front and an upside down V painted on their back so the drivers could tell at a distance which way a tram on the same track was heading. The painter, bemused by the way the fronts and backs of the trams looked so much alike, painted one of them the wrong way around, to the considerable confusion of the traffic staff the following day! The appearance of the trams, with their chimneys sticking up through the roof, sometimes earned them the nickname of 'pie carts'.

The other tropical tramway, at Broome, grew out of a typical Western Australian jetty tramway linking the ships with the town. These were really light railways and were equipped as such, but in Broome there was the added refinement of the provision of a half-hourly town service. Horse power was replaced by steam in 1910; the little locomotives made no pretence of looking like trams. Thomas Wood, in his book *Cobbers*, gives a brief but vivid impression of the Broome tramway as he saw it in 1931:

> An engine, and a truck whose bleached unpainted timbers looked like salvage from a galleon, steered along the jetty, crossed the foreshore, and after a mile of indecision stopped for good alongside a shed. Nothing else was in sight but sand and tussocky grass. Friendly souls explained that she was only doing the short trip today, being Sunday, but the town wasn't more than half a mile off. Straight up the street. And the Pearling Inspector lived in the house with the hedge. I couldn't miss it.[4]

After the Japanese attack on the town in March 1942 most people left for fear of an invasion and much was destroyed to prevent its being of use to the enemy. The tramway thus became an innocent victim of the war, the only Australian tramway to suffer in this manner.

Drama could strike even a small tramway, such as the one at Zeehan, in Tasmania, where a passenger service mixed in with extensive mine operations:

> On Saturday afternoon a runaway truck was seen rushing with terrific speed along Grubb's tramway towards Zeehan.
>
> To save the passenger car on the line the points were turned to lead the rushing truck into Davis' tramway shed, but this was directly into a load of dynamite.
>
> The truck was, however, too fast and jumped the points and went between the car and the dynamite, one foot only separating it from 150 cases of dynamite, the explosion of which would have been enough to destroy the town.[5]

In the sugarcane growing areas the visitor may often come across narrow gauge rail lines beside the road and signs warning of 'Tram'. These are used by the little trains (or trams as they are called) that take the cut cane to the mills. At Nambour they run, in the season, through the centre of the town down the middle of one of the streets. A story is told in Queensland of the English migrant who, seeing the Tram sign beside the road, waited for hours and hours, hoping to catch the next one to come along.

7

The Management and the Union

Among the people who operate the trams there are all different types. There are drivers who are fast or impatient, who take corners at speed to send little old ladies flying; there are those whose driving style causes flats on the wheels; or there are those who are slow, who are timid in traffic, always running late and being short shunted. There are conductors who are morose and those who are gregarious. But all but a few of these people have it in common that they staunchly support the union. The management has seemed, on the other hand, perhaps because of the very nature of the business, to be rigid and inflexible. The accommodations reached between management and staff have sometimes been difficult, and the transport unions have a long tradition of militancy.

In 1882 Francis Clapp spelt out the conditions under which his men worked: 'The hours of our 'bus drivers since we made the recent concession amount to ten hours and a half per day, taking one day with the other through the year'. This compared favourably with many overseas cities, but in particular with Manchester, Liverpool and San Francisco, where the average day's work on the buses was 14 hours.

> Of those ten hours and a half that our drivers have, they are forty-five minutes in the stable preparatory to starting, and at night counting the cash-box . . .'
>
> The wages of our Company for drivers are from 37 *s.* 6*d.* for spare drivers, relief men, to 50 *s.* for regular men, or an average of 42 *s.* 6 *d.* per week.

For comparison, the Manchester and Liverpool men earned between 32 and 35 shillings a week.

> The Company allow fifty-eight minutes to eighty minutes for meals; that is, a long day they have three reliefs from fifty-eight to eighty minutes. That you will understand, one trip; upon some of our lines it takes eighty minutes for a round trip, in others fifty-eight minutes.[1]

Whatever Francis Clapp thought of the equity of his system, the Victorian parliament legislated to oblige him to give his employees an eight-hour day and to pay overtime for work up to a maximum of 60 hours a week. Clapp interpreted this to mean that all his employees should work a 60 hour week. One thing

Tramway men march in Barrack Street by the Weld Club, 1910. *(Battye Library)*

'Strictly No Admittance'. Workmen closing up the team barn during the strike, 1910. *(Battye Library)*

Cable tram workshop, 1925; trams and buses being built. *(MMTB)*

Conductor on the footboard, Sydney, 1938. The blinds are down against the rain, but the conductor cannot avoid it. *(John Fairfax Ltd)*

the company was not going to stand was the formation of a union, and in 1885 Clapp sacked 36 bus drivers who had done just that. Most of the drivers then went out on a token strike. Clapp was persuaded to give the men every second Sunday off, but he refused to recognise the union, ruthlessly sacking its key members until it was driven underground. In its place he sponsored a benefit-society-union, partly supported by the company's funds. It soon became plain, especially when the union was refused permission to affiliate with the Trades Hall Council, that it was nothing but a creature of the company. Incensed, the men took control of the executive and made a proper union out of it. As the company retaliated by showing favouritism to non-unionists, a strike was called in support of the demand that all new recruits should join the union. For three days in mid February 1888 half of the trams were off the road, while the others were jeered in the streets. Francis Clapp, not one to waste time, hired strikebreakers in large numbers; the Trades Hall Council recommended a return to work to save the union and the strike collapsed. In an atmosphere of great bitterness, the committee refused to submit to the company, and 200 of its strongest supporters never worked on the trams in Melbourne again.

There was a strike in Brisbane in 1887 over

Preston workshops, 1976. *(Herald and Weekly Times)*

recognition of the union and the scale of wages and hours. Trams that were manhandled out on the streets through the picket lines were manned by volunteers, many of whom then found that they had a lot of difficulty with the tram horses. One volunteer conductor, having made it through to Woolloongabba, decided that he and the takings could make a better life elsewhere.

At this time there was a greater expectation of dishonesty among tramway employees than of dishonesty among the public in not paying fares. In Melbourne a bell punch was used to clip a numbered square on a strip of coloured card that the conductor had pinned to his uniform. The passenger did not receive a ticket, but had to take note of the ringing of the punch. The section punched out was retained in the body of the punch, and the number of fares taken was recorded on a dial inside. On return to the depot, the punch was checked by a pedantic gentleman to ensure that the money collected tallied with the little pieces of punched-out card, and with the tally on the dial.

Francis Clapp lived in Domain Road in a large house with a good view and an excellent stable of horses. Although at times his authoritarian personality made him a bit hard to get on with, he had his beloved tramways close to his heart. Although a sponsor of electric systems in other cities, he firmly believed in Melbourne's cables:

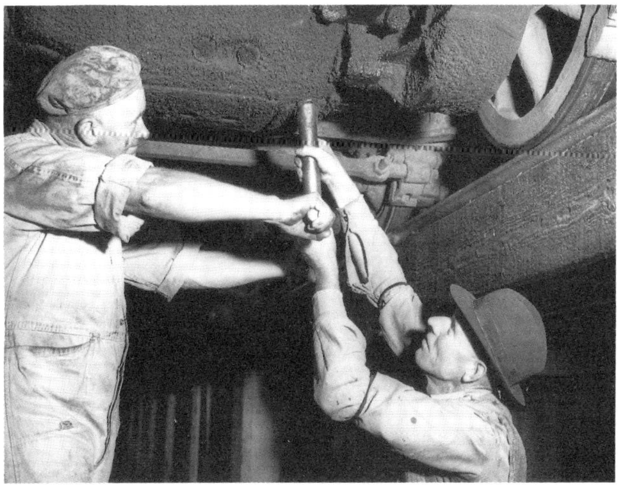

Working in the pit, Geelong. *(SEC)*

> The fact is generally overlooked that when in 1883 the enterprise of the company led to the adoption of the cable system for Melbourne, it was the best known at the time, electric tramways being then few, crude, and experimental. Melbourne at once took a foremost place among the cities of the world in traction matters. Since then electricity has been very much improved as a motive power, and because of their greater cheapness in construction and adaptability for light traffic, extensions

of lines, &c., electric tramways have now generally superseded other systems. But for places with heavy traffic cable tramways hold their own in cost of working, under similar conditions; and certainly our tramways give the public as good a service as is given by electric lines in other cities.[2]

When the crash came and people were starving in the streets of Melbourne, Clapp husbanded the company's resources, never closing down an unprofitable line, and looking to the future. Every penny had to count. Salaries were cut five times, between 1891 and 1894. The gripman who received £2 12 *s.* 0 *d.* per week was reduced to £2 0 s. 5 d., and the conductor from £2 10 *s.* 0 *d.* to £1 18 *s.* 6 *d.* Clapp reduced his own salary by a third. Men with second jobs, even men whose wives ran a small business, could not expect to be employed in these hard times, in preference to men with no other means of support. Inspectors kept an often minute check on the conductors to make sure that no fares found their way into private pockets. The company weathered the storm, but at a not insignificant cost in the goodwill of its employees. When the whole matter became the subject of a royal commission in 1898, few men had the courage of Francis Beaurepaire to give evidence.

Before giving my evidence before the Commission I went all round to my fellow employés and asked whether they were going to give evidence, but I could not get any one else to go. None of the single men would go, so they asked me if I would go. They were afraid of being discharged by the company.[3]

The main sources of grievance were the length of working hours, the low wages, the non-payment of special rates for overtime, the irregularity of meal hours, some forms of unfair treatment, and a variety of small matters such as the effect on the men's health of standing all day at the gripper, exposed to all weathers, and the system of 'spotters' who could accuse a man anonymously of breaches of the company's regulations.

After taking reams of evidence and sitting over lengthy deliberations, the commission determined that the men should have a 48-hour week, be paid for overtime and have regular mealtimes. In the matter of wages, they relied on Mr Clapp's assurances that these would be reviewed in the light of future company prosperity, as indeed they were, for the time would come when the men would receive bonus payments each year in line with profits — a situation that accorded well with Clapp's idea of how a company should be run.

Sydney also suffered an espionage system which attempted to ensure that a conductor could not sell the same ticket twice. In July 1908 two policemen on their first day caught out conductor Harold Croucher, who was summarily dismissed. The railway commissioners were as adamant on their side as the union was on its own, about what should be done, and as a result a strike was voted by a huge majority. Hearing that the men intended to stop work at midday of the Friday, the management ordered all trams back in their depots at 11. Not to be outdone, the unionists

Joseph Badger. *(Oxley Library)*

Troopers keep back the crowds at the start of the tram strike, 1908. *(Town and Country Journal)*

Police escort the steam motor as it tows the trams away. *(Town and Country Journal)*

spread the word and at 10 a.m., all over the city, the trams stopped dead. Extra police had been brought in from the country and the clerks trained to drive the trams, but ugly scenes ensued in George Street as the first office worker attempted to start the first of a great line of stranded vehicles. Mounted troopers appeared; arrests were made; the tram moved off. As the power station workers became involved, the electricity supply began to fail and the streets echoed to the half-forgotten sounds of steam whistles as the old steam tram motors were brought out to tow the long lines of electric cars home. Huge crowds booed and jeered. At the weekend the union rallied 70 000 people in Hyde Park, but the reality dawned on Monday when a few trams were out, manned by strikebreakers. By Wednesday the strike had totally collapsed, another to leave its legacy of bitterness for the future. Two years later it was Perth's turn.

The London-based Perth Electric Tramways Ltd had never managed anything more than a very modest profit, and the directors were quite unsympathetic to the men's demands for extra overtime payments. By Sunday 24 July 1910 all Perth trams had stopped and the union, in preparation for a long campaign, warned against the licensing of any new tram drivers in either Perth or Fremantle. The big shops in the city were the first to feel the pinch of their absent customers, but the people were also very annoyed by Australia's first really long tram strike. The residents of Subiaco even sought a writ of mandamus to compel the company to operate trams as provided under the terms of its franchise. With the men adamant on one side and the London directors on the other, the Company could not oblige. Mr Somerville, the manager, endeavoured to offer the men conditions similar to those in operation on the Municipal Tramways at Fremantle, but in vain. While the strikers pulled in their belts and their families started to go hungry, they waited on a court case which would indicate whether justice was on their side.

The test case involved motorman William Laidler, who sued the Company for £6 10 *s.* 7 *d.* overtime for the two weeks to 10 July. 'The plaintiff stated that from the time of reporting himself on duty he had been at the disposal of the company for 174 hours during the 13 days ended July 10, but received only 42 hours' work.'[4] He had been paid for the 42 hours but not for the remainder. The catch was that, as a casual worker, his terms of employment were not the same as those of the permanent men, as he might be required to attend for up to ten hours a day and only be paid the usual shilling an hour for the time he was out with a tram. His case, and a similar one brought by John Byfield a few days later, were dismissed with costs. The union, deciding that enough was enough, stated that it would permit the men to return to work on an individual basis if they wished. The men thereupon dissolved the union.

The company now decided to break the strike and the Perth council issued 36 new licenses for tram crew. On 18 August six trams came out of the barn to a large and vigorous demonstration by the strikers. Although they carried plain-clothes police, the drivers were greeted with 'rotten eggs and offensive epithets'.[5] Mounted troopers soon rode in to scatter the crowds. The strike dragged on until early September, by which time both sides were prepared to offer concessions. Mr Justice Burnside eventually ruled that, as from 1 January 1911, 'a day shall comprise between 12 consecutive hours. After the worker shall have

'What is the matter?' The tram strike has started. *(Town and Country Journal)*

Specials parade in Market Square, 1912. *(Oxley Library)*

completed ten hours in any one day, excluding meal times, he will be paid overtime at the rate of time and a quarter'.[6]

The company had the penultimate word when it stated that, on the 3 January holiday, it found itself unable to provide an adequate service because of the court's new overtime provisions, which obliged them to leave 15 cars idle at the barn. The last word was with the Western Australian government, which took over the whole system in May 1912.

In Brisbane the managerial style of Joseph Badger was due to run into trouble sooner or later, and it came in 1912. He was arrogant, astute and, like Francis Clapp, paternalistic. He lived in pleasant surroundings near the Toowong tram terminus, where the line had been built for his convenience, and from which steps led up to his backyard. Every morning tram No.100 would arrive to take him to work. In the best American tradition, this was his 'palace car', fitted with carpets, fancy seat covers, brass chandeliers and an ornately painted ceiling. As it progressed towards the city the lesser executives would be picked up; usually the closer to the city they lived, the less their rank.

In 1911 trouble began to loom when a Brisbane chapter of the Tramways Employees' Association was formed and Badger forbade the wearing by the tramwaymen of their union badges. The union decided to take the matter to arbitration but agitators of militant labour, sensing an issue for the elections due in March 1912, aroused the men to confrontation. From midday on 19 January the men would wear their badges in defiance of the company. The men involved were immediately removed from the trams and each had a personal interview with Badger during which he was invited to remove the badge or be suspended. Most chose suspension. Services struggled along on a skeleton basis while the summer humidity shortened everyone's tempers. The Labor Federation moved next to bring on a major escalation, a general strike. On Tuesday 30 January, 20 000 unionists in 43 unions stopped work at 6 p.m. At the tramway powerhouse, the men had already gone out, but still the service limped along. Angry strikers took the city closer to anarchy by derailing a tram at Red Hill and placing dynamite in the points where it was hoped to blow up a heavily loaded tram from Bulimba Ferry. Luckily for the loss of life which might have ensued, the dynamite failed to explode, but for safety, all services were suspended indefinitely.

On the same day, after an attempt on the life of a

prominent police officer and with the Trades Hall issuing its own currency and forcing shopkeepers to accept it, the premier, Digby Denham, asked the federal government for troops. They were refused. In their absence, the ghost of the old pre-Federation Queensland army was invoked, with hundreds of special constables sworn in and armed with batons. A show of strength was planned for what became known as Black Friday. A big demonstration had been planned for that day in Market Square, but the strikers were met by a small army of mounted and foot police armed with batons and bayonets. Stones flew, the troopers charged, batons flashed and cracked in the sunlight as strikers and bystanders together were scattered. One woman who had been making inflammatory speeches stuck a hatpin into the horse ridden by the commissioner of police, Major Cahill. He was badly thrown and lamed for life.

From then on, Brisbane saw a regular morning muster of police and specials until, on 5 February, the city was considered pacified enough for tram services to begin again. Twelve cars ran from the Valley to Vulture Street, through streets where every intersection was heavily guarded. Joseph Badger was victorious.

The strike dragged on in other parts of Queensland for another month until the employers agreed not to victimise those who were prepared to return to work, and although the Arbitration Court found in favour of the unionists' right to wear their badges, no striker was employed again by the Brisbane Tramway Company. On the other hand, many people would for years afterwards step back and let a tram go by if they saw it was crewed by someone who had helped break the general strike.

Sydney suffered another major strike in August 1917, but services were maintained on the main lines on a skeleton basis by men who did not agree with the Union's stand, and by clerical staff. As the strike spread to other areas and to other trades, the government was able to label the strikers as traitors to the cause of Britain and her allies in the Great War, and much bitterness ensued. A two week strike in Sydney became a seven week strike in Broken Hill, and the parlous financial situation of the provincial tramway was further affected by lengthy strikes in the mines during 1919 and 1920. These troubles, as well as an uncertain future in population and employment in the city, signalled an early demise for the Broken Hill tramways.

Other countries were affected by strikes. In New Zealand, a strike in Christchurch in 1932 actually resulted in the death of a tramwayman.

A tradition of militancy remained with the tramways, and at times of social strain, such as the years after the Second World War, there were many strikes and stoppages. In Melbourne in 1969, the union leader Clarrie O'Shea was even gaoled. The union refused to pay a fine imposed by the courts, and the government of Henry Bolte took strong action. 'All bosses are bastards,' said Clarrie O'Shea.[7]

8

Something New

By the 1920s the austerity of the Great War was over and society was looking for something new. The motor car was beginning to make an impact, as was illustrated by the joke about the man who, on finding a piece of rubber tyre in his pie, observed that the car was replacing the horse everywhere nowadays. Transport in Australia's four largest cities was also changing.

Melbourne, it sometimes seemed, had the furthest to go, retaining as it did a cable tram system bigger than all those in the rest of the world put together. To the Sydney eye in particular, the cable trams made Melbourne seem conservative and quaint. Sydney, to a visitor of Biblical bent, and not used to the pace, was the city of the quick and the dead — if you were not quick you were dead — and it was not for nothing that it was said of someone who made a hurried getaway that 'He shot through like a Bondi tram'.

(Many attempts have been made to find the origin of this quintessential Sydney expression in the steam trams, but I believe it is more complex. In the 1890s to 'do a Bondi' meant to beat someone up, and an attacker would often hit and then run. The accretion of the tram to the phrase would have occurred at some later time, probably as a result of simple rhyming slang — scram/tram. It is most unlikely that any tram demonstrated a speed such as would enshrine it as a criterion in colloquial speech. First literary mention is recorded as 1945.)

Melbourne saw its first inner suburban electric trams on 5 May 1906 as a result of the land speculations of the premier, Thomas Bent, who arranged for the Victorian Railways to construct an 'electric street railway' from St Kilda station to Brighton. Vacant land along the route was now not only adjacent to some pleasant beaches, but also well provided with a fast transport service to the city, and therefore ripe for development. Bent claimed to have been pushing for this tramway for 23 years, but the result was a first rate tramway with 'handsome vehicles, far superior in appearance to those in use in Sydney, and not so high from the ground level'.[1] One incident of the opening day involved a patriot who believed the trams should have been built in Australia, and defaced the J. G. Brill & Co builder's plate. In October of the same year the North Melbourne Electric Tramway and Lighting Company Ltd opened its electric lines on the other side of the city. Services ran from the cable tram terminus at Flemington Bridge to Essendon and the Saltwater River.

Railway Square. *(postcard)*

Disaster struck the Brighton line less than a year after it had opened when the car shed and all 17 trams were destroyed by fire. The railway workshops worked night and day to have the line back in service after only ten days, mainly by using former Sydney trams that had become too small to be useful. High-floored and narrow, they were never popular in Melbourne.

As the years went on, all the suburbs saw the establishment of electric tramways around the perimeter of the cable system. They were a great improvement on the horsecars which had fed passengers into the ends of the cable tramways at several points. People would still have to change from the electric car to the cable car to complete their journeys in most cases, but in 1916 the Hawthorn Tramways Trust was the first to penetrate to the edge of the city with its terminus at Princes Bridge in Batman Avenue. At the other end of the line, in 55 hectares of rolling bushland, was Wattle Park, a

Pride of the city, a streamlined tram, 1940. *(BTMS)*

Prototype P-class tram, designed in 1916, built in 1921. *(C. Jones collection)*

pleasant area with sports grounds and picnic places. This trolley park was developed and operated by the tramways and remains the last of its kind in the world. It is even still possible to indulge in the old-fashioned pleasure of hearing recitals under the trees by the Tramways Band.

The suburban electric tramways evolved a type of tram unique to Australia, a type that was copied in Sydney, Brisbane and Adelaide, the bogie drop-centre tram. The first of these, built at the Adelaide works of Duncan and Fraser, went into service for the Prahran and Malvern Tramways Trust in 1913. Roomy, robust and popular, it was chosen to become the standard Melbourne tram in 1923 and some of the originals were still in commercial operation in Ballarat and Bendigo almost 60 years after they were built.

In 1916, at the age of 83, Francis Clapp relinquished control of his cable tramways to a governmental body, and in 1919 a new organisation was established to take over all of Melbourne's tramways except for those operated by the Victorian Railways. This was the Melbourne and Metropolitan Tramways Board. Although committed to the eventual

Very un-Australian—two only of this New York-style 'stepless' car were imported, one for Brisbane and one for Perth. They entered service in 1914. *(Oxley Library)*

conversion of all the cable lines to electricity, one of the first things the new board had to do was to build more cable trams. The system was, in fact, at its peak in 1925, when over 148 million fares were sold on the cable cars. The trams had become a great competitor with the railways in the suburbs and their popularity was one of the reasons behind the electrification of the Melbourne suburban railways between 1919 and 1926. In their turn the trams had to be modernised, not into a motor bus or a trolley bus system, but into the best electric tramway system that could be built. The General Scheme for the Future Development of Tramways, one of the most comprehensive plans ever devised in Australia for urban transport, was adopted by the Victorian parliament in 1923.

One by one the cable-car lines were cut back and the electric cars came closer to the centre of the city. By 1926 the electric trams were running the length of the noble boulevard of St Kilda Road, shining in their new green paintwork to match the trees. Collins Street was converted in 1929. Many people regretted the passing of the cable cars. They remembered riding in the open on the front of the dummy on a warm summer evening; the sound of their bells, which to a country visitor arriving at Spencer Street Station, spoke immediately of Melbourne; their gentle unassuming ways, and the silent mechanical marvel of their very existence.

Later closures were often marked with wild hooliganism, as the Argus reported in 1937:

> Six trams were damaged with fusillades of road metal and by souvenir hunters when the South Melbourne and Port Melbourne cable trams were run on Saturday night for the last time.
>
> Overloading caused one tram trailer to bolt and set fire to a dummy. One tram in particular suffered. Almost all its windows were broken with stones, every moveable part was taken away, and woodwork was torn off . . .

Dandenong Road. *(postcard)*

Trams and crowds in Pitt Street. *(C. Jones collection)*

Circular Quay. *(postcard)*

> Serious injury might have occurred when the last South Melbourne tram was shunting at the city terminus at the corner of Collins and Market streets a few minutes after midnight. The brakes on the trailer, which was much overladen, did not hold it, and as it ran for 15 yards downhill toward the dummy passengers and spectators shouted warnings to several persons who were standing near the dummy. Men and youths leaped to safety before the trailer crashed into the back of the dummy. The ironwork of the dummy was bent, but the tram was not severely damaged . . .
>
> After the closing doors of the shed had hidden the last cable trams to run south of the Yarra the crowd dispersed. Many carried away souvenirs, including a wire guard and a large portion of a door. One youth was charged at the Port Melbourne watchhouse with having been illegally in possession of a destination sign.[2]

Tram posed at Elwood, 1922. *(C. Jones collection)*

In Brisbane the troubled affairs of the Brisbane Tramway company were coming to an end. The advent of a new Labor government in 1915 saw it once more under attack as a wicked monopoly run by 'a foreign industrial tyrant'.[3] An embattled Joseph Badger, faced with the expiry of the company's franchise in 1920, endeavoured to obtain municipal support for its extension, but without success. As a result he resolved to cease new investment in track extensions and the system started to become run down. The Queensland government twice introduced legislation for the compulsory purchase of the tramways prior to 1920, but outside pressure forced it to back down. Finally in 1923 the Brisbane tramways came under the control of the Brisbane Tramway Trust.

Opening day, Elsternwick, 1913. *(postcard)*

Birney Tram at Charing Cross, 1971. *(C. Jones)*

A Baby Dreadnought tram, built in 1943 with the not unusual expedient of recycling old equipment. *(C. Jones)*

A wreath for the end of the Clovelly line, 1957. *(TMSV)*

R1-class tram, Elizabeth Street, 1961. *(C. Jones)*

Trams at Treasury. *(C. Jones)*

Trams at Victoria Bridge. *(D. Jones)*

Quiet afternoon at Acland Street. *(C. Jones)*

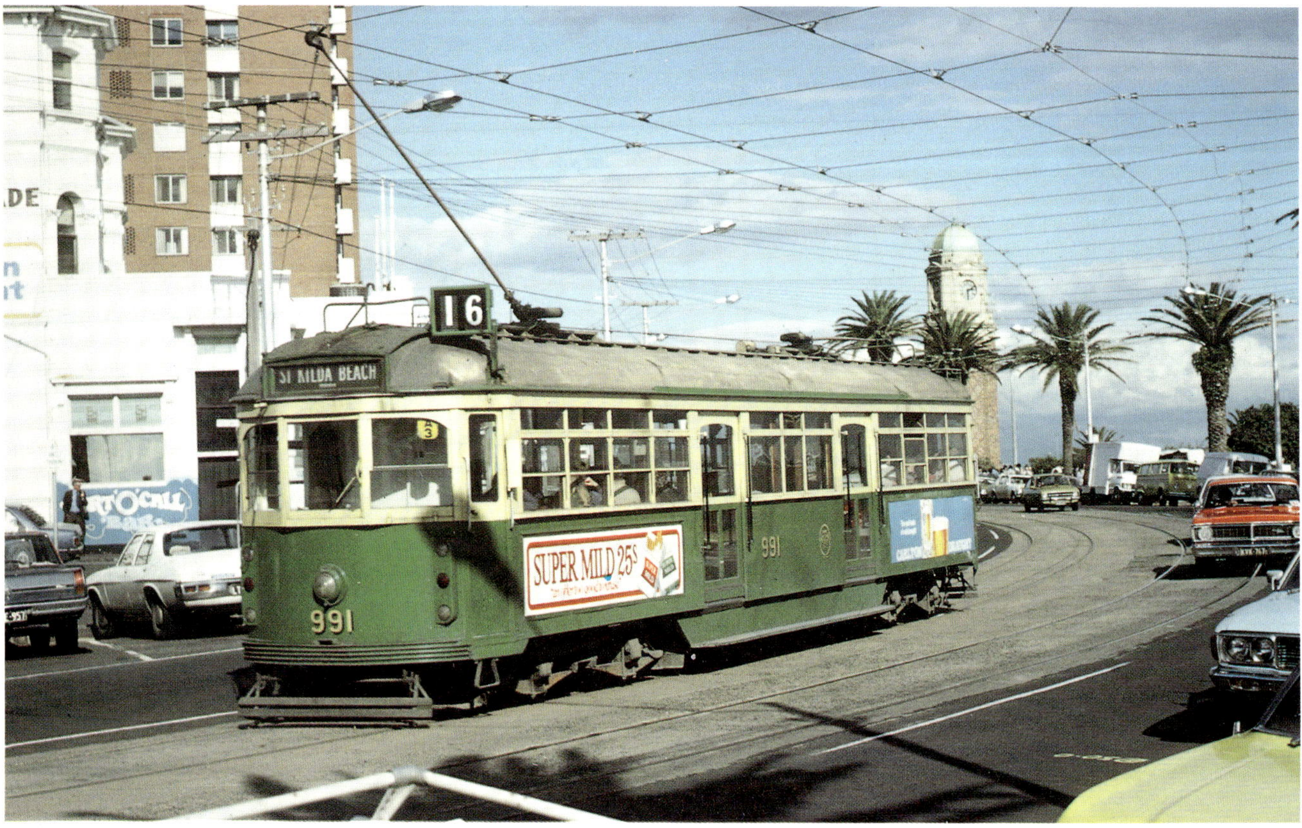

Tram on the Esplanade. *(C. Jones)*

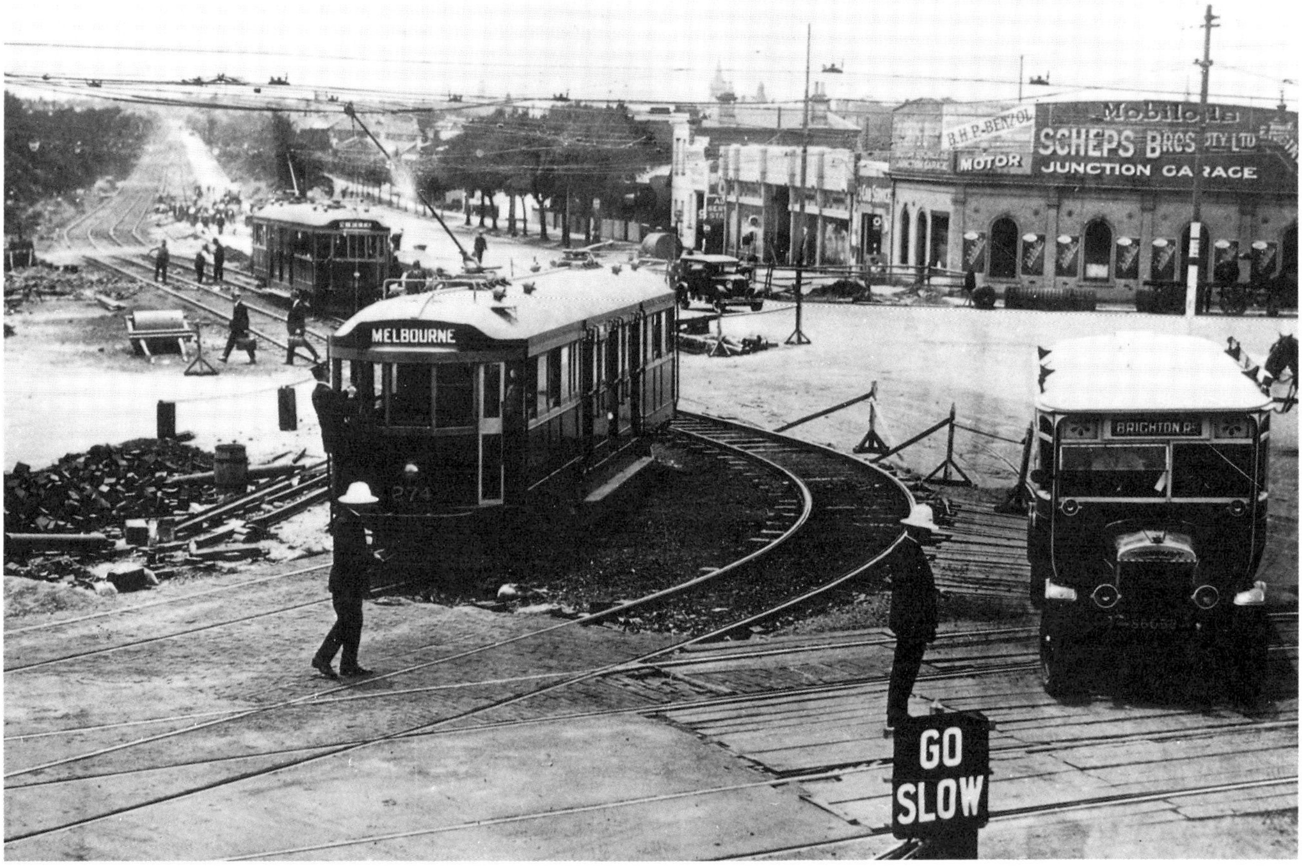

New electric tramway under construction at St Kilda Junction and St Kilda Road. *(MMTB)*

Collins Street, the most beautiful street in Australia. *(postcard)*

Museum bound, an E-class set swings into Elizabeth Street from Bathurst Street by the Hyde Park Hotel on an enthusiast tour, 1955. *(Mitchell Library)*

Tram in Barrack Street. *(W.A. Government Printer)*

The Trust set about a vigorous program of new construction, and in its brief three years it presided over the opening of no fewer than seven extensions to existing routes and one new branch line. Initially, new tramcar construction was limited to the well-tried 'dreadnought' design — an open bogie saloon car of the type known in some parts of the world as a jardinière. However 1925 saw the first of the drop-centre trams on the road. These trams, which set a new standard in Brisbane, were largely designed by the Sydney tramway authorities.

The big event in the Brisbane of the 1920s was the formation of the Greater Brisbane Council. A long tradition of municipal inertia and misgovernment was ended by the combination of 20 cities, towns and shires in 1925 to form the Brisbane City Council. Under a council of 24 aldermen sitting as government and opposition, and a mayor elected by the popular vote of the whole city, Brisbane covered an area of 97 124 hectares. One of the major utilities which passed into the care of the new council was the tramways, which had the great good fortune to attract two excellent administrators in George Steer and Sydney Quinn. As secretary, Sydney Quinn's hand guided the Tramway Trust and then the council's Transport Department from 1923 until he succeeded George Steer as general manager in 1939. He finally retired from the service in 1953, after which he held an advisory post for another three years.

Along with regular track extensions to keep pace

The classical drop-centre tram, a W2 class posed in 1929, newly converted. *(MMTB)*

with the expanding suburbs, Steer and Quinn provided a new type of tram, based on the most recent Melbourne equipment but designed for Brisbane conditions, which rolled out, streamlined, silver and magnificent, onto the streets from 1938.

Sydney was the tramway city par excellence. In the 1920s something of the order of 325 million fares would be sold each year by conductors hanging off the footboards of the big crossbench cars. One could go almost anywhere by tram. From the north-western extremity of the system at Ryde station one could, given sufficient time and enthusiasm, ride over 50

Tram at Milsons Point. *(postcard)*

Tram climbing Boomerang Street from Woolloomooloo. *(LaTrobe Library)*

kilometres by tram, via the city and North Sydney to Narrabeen, with two short ferry crossings between isolated sections. La Perouse, on the southern extremity, was almost 18 kilometres by tram from Circular Quay. It was an impressive service at any time, but never more so than when it had to shift crowds; when a big ferry such as the *Kuttabul* could disgorge 2600 passengers from North Sydney at Circular Quay in the morning peak and they would swarm aboard the waiting trams which would then clang their way towards shop and office in Pitt Street, or George Street, or Elizabeth Street. Just over 2.5 kilometres away, at Central Railway, the same scene would be repeated as the commuter trains poured their passengers onto what John Bradfield once described as the 'moving platform' of trams to go downtown. In the one-way thoroughfares of Pitt and Castlereagh Streets, peak-hour trams would be carrying a phenomenal 25 000 people per hour. At Randwick on race days the trams would pull in to a regular railway station with six platforms as well as overhead bridges to control the crowds. In the 1920s as many as 480 trams might be required to carry the great surge of humanity after the last race. It was no wonder that one of the events of the spring racing season was named the Tramway Handicap.

Among the Sydney tram depots, that at Dowling Street was far the largest, and indeed one of the largest in the world. At its peak in the 1940s, it accommodated 327 tramcars, with a traffic staff of over 1000.

Unlike Melbourne, Sydney could never boast wide

O class for Coogee, 1913. *(Mitchell Library)*

O class, Elizabeth Street, 1953. *(LaTrobe Library)*

straight streets. Very often there would be no room to park on one side of the road because of the double lines of tramway. The situation was particularly bad between St Peters and Tempe on what is now the Princes Highway. Tram passengers could step straight onto the footpath on one side, while slow-moving lorries and waggons had to make way for the trams by moving right over to the other side of the road. Inevitably, as other vehicular traffic grew, the roads became congested and services were slowed. Even when the inevitable road-widening took place, the traffic was often found to have grown in volume so much that the trams seemed to be constant large, imperious and trackbound competitors.

The Sydney tramways had their own curiosities to intrigue the visitor, and the first among these were the cabbalistic symbols that appeared with the destination: a big red cross for Abbotsford, two red dots for Glebe Point, three green diamonds for Canterbury, two green dots for Marrickville, and so on. Mysterious to the uninitiated, they were familiar to the Sydneysider and, as shorthand for the routes, they gained for the areas in which they were used the nicknames of the green lines or the red lines. They even inspired a poem by R.G. Henderson which was published in *The Bulletin*:

Three Green Diamonds

Three green diamonds, flying up the street,
Three green diamonds, glamorous and fleet!
Threepence worth of magic and the kindness of fate
And three green diamonds took me to Kitty's gate.

Gone are those years, but still the wonder stays,
Giving some colour to dull working days;
The others are but trams and I give them not a glance,
But the three green diamonds are the blazon of romance.[4]

Sydney had some very steep tramlines, with 1 in 11 as the usual maximum gradient. At Neutral Bay and Balmain, however, the steep approaches to the ferry wharves demanded special measures. Trams on the Neutral Bay line had to have special brakes, but to make the 1 in 8.25 descent of Darling Street at

Elizabeth Street. *(postcard)*

Trams at North Bondi terminus, 1957. *(National Library)*

Balmain the trams used a counterweight. This was operated under the road on a cable. The tram, coming down the hill, would nose up to the counterweight car, which would offer sufficient resistance for ordinary braking to be used safely. Going up the hill, the counterweight would exert its gentle pressure behind the tram.

Sydney shared with Port Adelaide the inconvenience of swing-span bridges over which the trams had to pass. There were two in Sydney: the Gladesville Bridge with a span of 37 metres, and the Glebe Island Bridge with a span of 58 metres. Sometimes, after opening for a ship, Sydney's Gladesville Bridge would not close on the exact alignment for the tram tracks, and the end of the line to Ryde would be isolated until the fault could be rectified. The Jervois Bridge in Port Adelaide could be similarly cranky.

A vehicle unique to Sydney was the prison tram, a very solid vehicle which carried convicted criminals from Darlinghurst Courthouse to Long Bay gaol. In 1946 Darcy Dugan and an accomplice escaped from this tram by cutting a hole in the roof.

At Watsons Bay the trams ran quite close to two of the forts that guarded Sydney Heads. In particular there was a 23-centimetre gun at Signal Hill, near the Pacific Hotel, and trams had to be careful not to be nearby when the guns were fired, or the blast might break all their windows.

The various strains on Sydney's public transport

Adelaide F1-class tram. *(STA)*

system could best be met, it was felt, by electrifying the existing suburban railways, by building an underground electric railway in the city area and by the construction of the North Shore Bridge, and the man who campaigned long and hard for these was John Bradfield. As early as 1899 an underground railway was planned, with a station at King Street and a possible branch to the eastern suburbs. Bradfield took up the idea and in 1911 he was recommending this

Double Truck Car for Melbourne and Metropolitan Tramway Board.

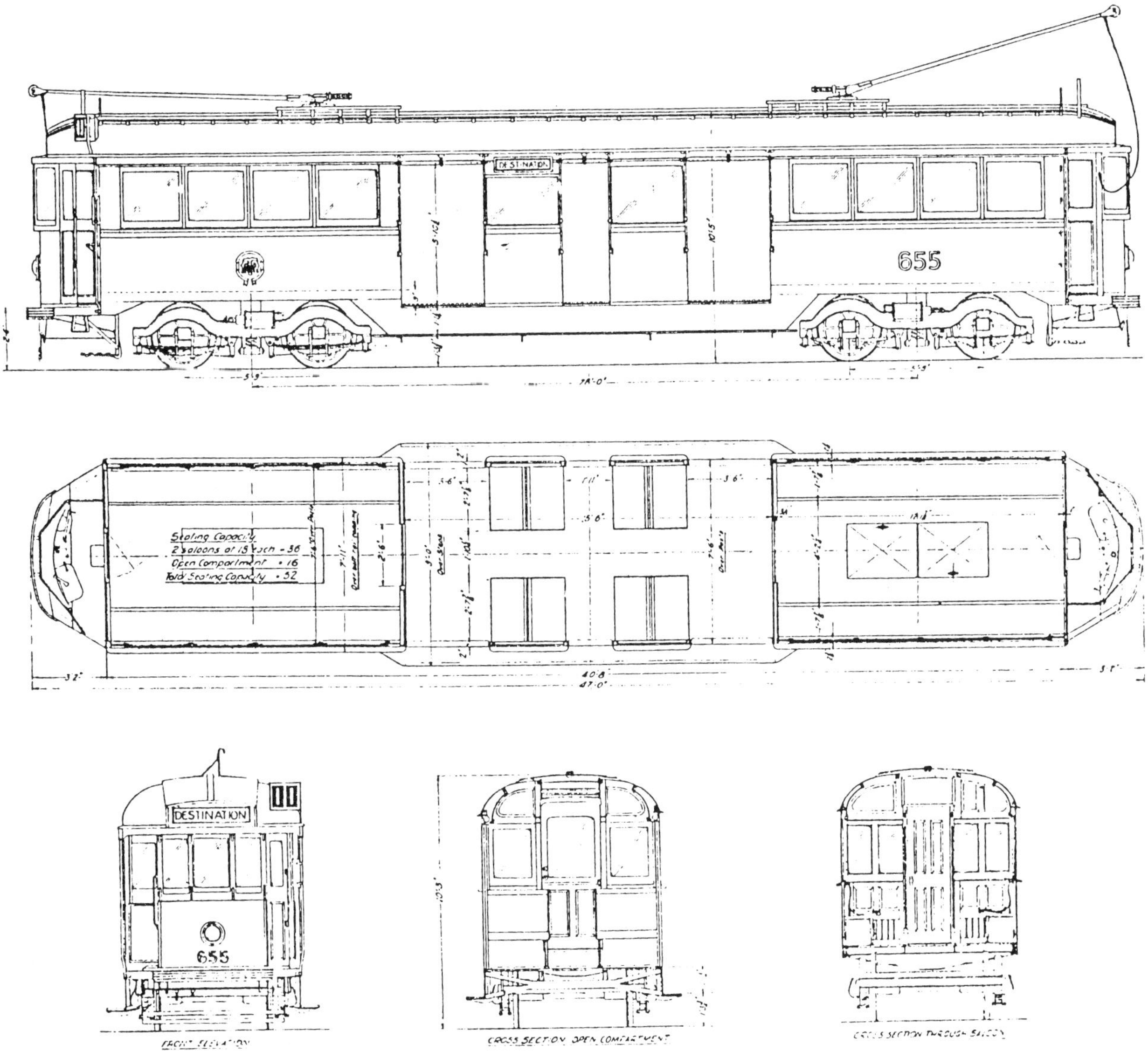

W3 class plan. *(The Tramway and Railway World)*

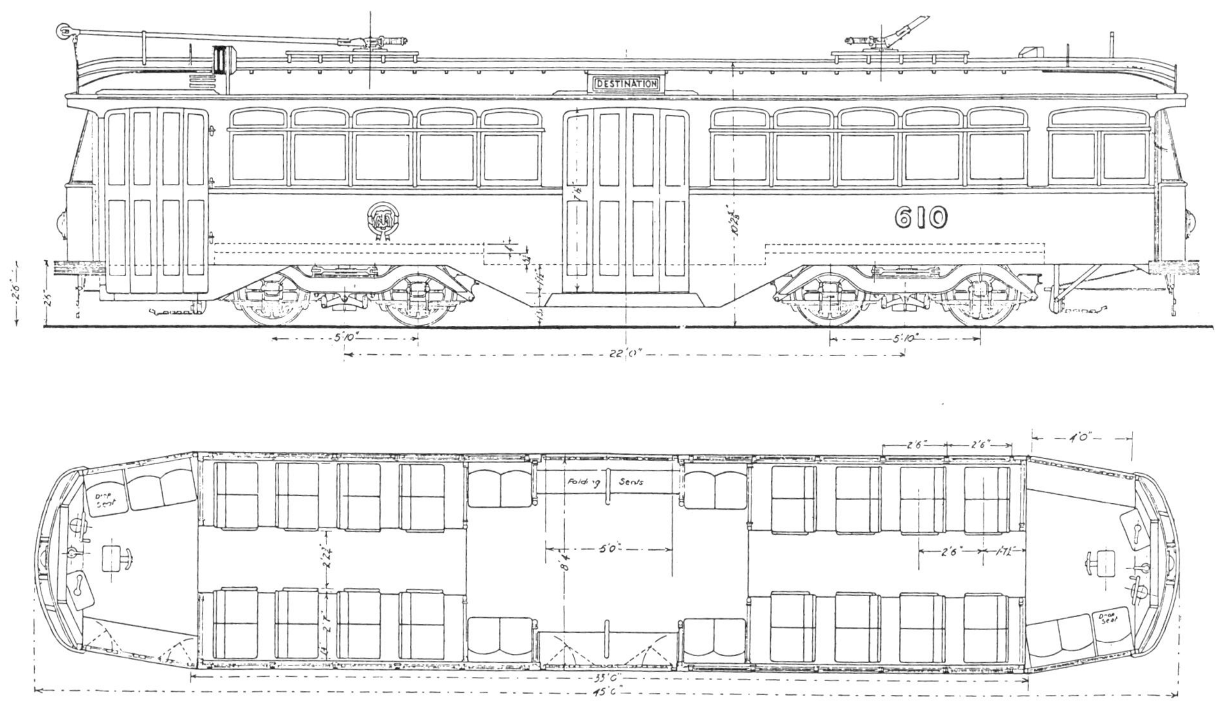

Elevation and Plan of the New Car of the Melbourne and Metropolitan Tramways Board, Victoria.

Y1 class plan. *(The Tramway and Railway World)*

solution. In 1924 his doctoral thesis at Sydney University was entitled 'The City and Suburban Electric Railways and the Sydney Harbour Bridge'. Bradfield's schemes were nothing if not grandiose, including substantial lengths of underground railway and two high-level bridges — one to the North Shore and one to Balmain. He even proposed that the majority of the tramways in the city should be placed in tunnels under Pitt and Castlereagh Streets, to have both the trams and the streets clear of congestion. The first part of his plan began to come true in 1926 with the running of the first electric trains and the opening of the first two stations of the City Railway.

> With spectators cheering, and the train whistle blowing 'cock-a-doodle-doos,' the first train to travel on the City Railway slid through the tunnels from Central Station into the glittering whiteness of Museum Station shortly after 10 o'clock . . .
>
> Red and green signal lights flicked like Morse lamps at each end of the platform, and frequently a hollow rumble came from the tunnels in the direction of the Central Station. A few moments later the train appeared, and the huge arched chamber echoed with cheers.[5]

The next great event was the opening of the Sydney Harbour Bridge itself in 1932. In place of two of the four railway tracks which it was to carry, the North Sydney trams were routed across the bridge to finish underground at Wynyard Station. It was to be Australia's only underground tramway.

The Sydney tramways reached their maximum electrified length of 264 kilometres in 1932 and in this confident climate a new tram design, the R-class, was introduced. It marked a significant change in comfort away from the universal crossbench designs, which, as a character in an Emile Mercier cartoon remarked, were far from warm, even though called toastracks, to the Melbourne style of drop-centre saloon. As in Melbourne, the new trams were painted a pleasant green. The Watsons Bay line, passing as it did through upper crust suburbs, was a prime candidate for the new trams. Supreme Court judges and other men of note who travelled on gold passes were regular commuters and became well known to the tram crews. Some conductors used to knock on their doors on the way out to the terminus to make sure that they would be ready when the tram returned on its way to the city, and for this they received their reward every Christmas.

Adelaide was also making its contribution to the modern age by the conversion of a steam railway to an electric tramway. It would have seemed curious, in the Adelaide of the 1920s, to see a steam locomotive with several carriages puffing up the middle of King William Street beside the tram lines to Victoria Square. Indeed, electrification of the Glenelg railway had been considered as far back as 1904. Although William Goodman, a few years later, was proposing heavy American-style interurban trams for the line, the government would not move to change the status quo. The Glenelg steam railway was leisurely and friendly.

Brisbane drop-centre tram, 1933. *(BTMS)*

Regular commuters had their own spots in the carriages. Electric trams, on the other hand, promised crowds, strap hanging, trampled feet and possible injury from hat pins! When William Goodman finally had his way in 1929, the new line was superb, a showpiece of how such things could be done. The big shining red interurban trams could run in coupled pairs down the straight tracks of their own right of way almost all the way from the city to Glenelg. The new line served Morphettville racecourse, and the Tramways Trust built a special horsebox trailer which could be towed behind a tram to and from the course. This unique service was christened by the great Phar Lap himself in May 1930.

Still run with its original stock, the Glenelg tramway is now the only Australian line left in commercial service outside Melbourne, and with it, Adelaide was able to celebrate a century of tramway operation in June 1978.

The following table gives typical passenger numbers carried annually by the principal Australian tramways in the 1920s[6]:

City	*Passengers*
Sydney	315 610 000
Melbourne	228 140 000
Brisbane	77 250 000
Adelaide	62 830 000
Perth	28 870 000
Newcastle	20 200 000
Hobart	10 280 000
Launceston	6 470 000
Kalgoorlie	5 140 000
Ballarat	4 010 000
Fremantle	3 070 000
Bendigo	2 450 000
Geelong	2 120 000
Rockhampton	1 780 000

9

Something Old

Trams had become the familiar of the people. In the 1920s there was scarcely a person in urban Australia, from whatever walk of life, who did not at some time travel on them. But like something taken too much for granted, the trams eventually became reliable but unnoticed, and their appearance, once smart and modern, became middle-aged and possibly unkempt. Poorly maintained, the woodwork of the more lightly constructed cars would creak and the motors grind. People turned from the faithful tram to a new love, the motor car. Private cars spread only slowly through the community, so at first the main impact of the motor vehicle was in the form of pirate buses, often quite small, that could follow the tram routes and pick up passengers waiting at the stops. In Adelaide the first answer to the pirate bus was to use the fastest trams as 'nark cars' to run ahead of the competitor and catch the passengers before he did. The type of tram used for this became known as a Desert Gold, after a contemporary racehorse. In other parts of the world the answer to the pirate bus, or jitney, was perhaps an improved type of tram, or a trolley bus, or perhaps complete capitulation and the closure of the tramway. In Australia the more usual solution was governmental control by licensing services. In a city such as Brisbane, buses almost died out. Here in the north, most of the old traditions still survived, such as the route of the new Grange tramline being different from that of the bus used to build up passenger demand, because of land speculation interests. The first tram on the line was welcomed in appropriate style by the orchestra of the local school. Land values soared when a new tramline was built.

At the same time, two of the three New South Wales provincial tramways were becoming a memory. The general scheme adopted by the New South Wales Railways was to introduce the latest technology first in Sydney, while the older style equipment could then be displaced to outer suburban locations and provincial cities. Newcastle obtained its steam trams after Sydney's had been established, but the great and rapid growth of the Sydney electric system up to the Great War left no spare capacity to commence electrification proposals in Newcastle. Indeed, it was necessary to build new steam motors at Randwick as late as 1923 to keep steam services going in the Newcastle area. Government steam tramways were established in Broken Hill in 1902 and Maitland in 1909, and had the department's resources not been strained to the extreme to provide for the demands of the metropolis, each might have followed Newcastle in receiving electric trams. As it was, electrification, when it came to Newcastle in 1923, was about 15 years behind schedule, the trams refurbished second-hand Sydney vehicles (as ever). The tramways in the other provincial cities were declared to be uneconomic and closed. Cities such as Lismore and Wollongong never saw trams at all.

Steam lingered in suburban Kogarah and Parramatta for some time after private buses had replaced several other lines. Even after the Parramatta ferry service closed in 1928 it was still possible to take a gritty ride down among the factories to Redbank. The mid morning mixed would clank to a halt in the centre of Parramatta, where a blast on the whistle would bring out all the shop assistants with cut lunches to be delivered to factory workers further down the line. Housewives similarly could have orders filled in town if they handed them to the conductor in the morning. This friendly service finally collapsed in the early years of the Second World War. Kogarah missed an entire era in the history of urban transport by replacing its steam trams, not with electric trams, but with trolley buses, in 1937.

Even horse trams lingered on in a few backwaters. At Beaumaris, the horse tram meandered down beside Port Phillip Bay, with its untended rails sticking up out of the sandy road, until 1915. In Melbourne it was possible to step back in time on the horse tram to the zoo until the police strike of 1923 when, during the general disturbances that racked the city, the car shed was burned and the service was never reinstated. In the South Australian outport of Moonta the horse trams worked along the main street until the Great Depression carried them away. These trams could still be seen, as late as the 1950s, patiently plodding along a short line between Victor Harbor and Granite Island.

A nice naval story is told from 1952:

OP-class car, newly converted, 1919. *(C. Jones collection)*

The LP class, the only type of electric tram operated in Newcastle. *(Newcastle Public Library)*

> My First Lieutenant and I were returning to the ship, by taxi, when we heard a number of voices chanting 'The Song of the Volga Boatmen'. On nearing the scene I was amused to see that my crew, returning to the ship after an obviously good run ashore, had decided that the horse must be tired and had put him inside the tram and were between the shafts of the tram and were proceeding merrily on their way. All was well until they reached the *Gladstone*. The horse had cocked his tail once or twice inside the tram and resisted all efforts to remove him by letting fly with his hind legs. The tram driver was sitting quietly smoking a cigarette inside the tram, quite oblivious to the chaos going on. Several of my 'boys' got hit by flying dung. Finally the driver got up and said to the horse 'Back boy', and the horse obediently backed out of the tram. My Executive Officer then ordered the sailors to run hoses from the ship and clean out the tram.[1]

By an odd turn of fate, the horse trams returned to Granite Island in June 1986. A crowd of 4 000 people were there to welcome two brand new horse trams, carefully modelled on the style of 1879, which recommenced the service. The drivers did not wear tramway uniforms, but bushmen's drizabones.

By the 1920s the tramways of the golden cities of Ballarat and Bendigo were starting to look tired and run down. The great mines were closing and prosperity was ebbing away. Another shadow on the horizon of the tramways was the State Electricity Commission, which would be able to purchase their parent Electric Supply Company in 1931 and merge its assets into a statewide power grid. The SEC was not enthusiastic about becoming a tramway operator, whereas the local councils were most insistent that the trams should be retained, though without their ruinous finances becoming a burden on the ratepayers. In the end the government legislated to pass the provincial tramways to the SEC, and a substantial amount of money from a National Recovery Fund was made available for their rehabilitation. Tracks were relaid and overhead wires replaced, and in the matter of new trams, there were a number of middle-aged ladies who had seen better days in Melbourne, who would be available for sale at a very reasonable price. From this time on, the Victorian provincial tramways always made do with second-hand vehicles, thus ensuring that a number of them would eventually find their way into a museum.

The trams of which the present-day Bendigo Trust is so proud are the Birney safety cars. Four of these came when the Port Adelaide tramways were closed, to join two already in Geelong; after the Geelong closure, all six went to Bendigo. The type originated in the difficulties experienced by a number of American tramway authorities after the Great War in maintaining viable services on lightly patronised lines. A type of small saloon tram was therefore designed

Newcastle trams, coupled. *(Newcastle Public Library)*

Trams in Queen Street, 1945. *(BTMS)*

Tram for Holland Park, 1945. *(Courier Mail)*

Victor Harbor tram. *(postcard)*

in the works of J. G. Brill which could be operated by one man. It was referred to as a safety car as it could not start until its door was closed and the step folded. Although widespread in its country of origin, few were imported into Australia. Melbourne had two, and the rest finished in Bendigo, where they may still delight the tourist on a journey from the gold mine to the joss house.[2]

Of the three SEC tramways, the Geelong system should have stood the best chance of survival. Although its trams had to have their ends painted with bright tiger stripes to make them more visible to motorists, they retained good levels of patronage until the end. The postwar world, however, was not an easy one for trams and they succumbed to an expert report and the desire of the operating authority to be rid of them. With the closure of Geelong in 1956, the curiosity was that Ballarat and Bendigo retained their trams for so long after. Perhaps it was because of the feeling, even then, that trams were what made a city, that the people of those two cities fought so hard for their retention. The trams became something of an end in themselves as they trundled their antique way along Pall Mall or Sturt Street. People didn't use them, but they still liked them. By the late 1960s, so few people would choose to use the tram instead of their cars that the old vehicles rolled around largely empty. It was time for them to go.[3]

And yet, they had become too much of a living museum to be thrown away entirely. In both cities, fortunately, there were enthusiasts prepared to preserve the trams as a museum. To assist them, the authorities left part of the street track intact, and in due course the trams that had become irrelevant as public transport ran again as a service for tourists.

The Great Depression hit New South Wales, if anything, harder than the other states. It might often happen that the tram fare was a luxury that could be avoided entirely by smartly avoiding the conductor on the open footboards. Tramway finances, as a result of motor bus competition, were becoming uncertain, resulting in the sacking of thousands of employees. Things were so bad by 1932 that the government resorted to that universal Australian solution, a royal

Broken Hill tram, 1902. *(BHP)*

Ballarat trams at the city terminus by the Town Hall. *(SEC)*

Geelong trams at T&G Corner. *(SEC)*

Not as good as the trams, a double-decker Leyland Titan bus in Bourke Street. *(postcard)*

commission. This resulted in the first closure of some short lines from 1933, but also in the introduction of a trolley bus service from the Town Hall to Potts Point. In the busy environment of William Street, the trolley bus was just one vehicle too many, while its overhead wiring, along with that for the trams, contributed significantly to what was seen at the best of times as an unsightly web. Although the steam trams at Kogarah were also replaced by trolley buses, this was Sydney's last flirtation with the new type of vehicle. Henceforth, the policy was that all trams would go, and in their place there would be double-deck motor buses. In 1933 the Department of Road Transport and Tramways was in the process of taking over private bus services, and in the course of this acquired its first double-deck motor buses, then only four years old. The cost of a bus was three quarters that of a tram; the bus was able to do without costly steel rails and overhead wires, and therefore its routes could be extended indefinitely or varied at will. Double-deck buses started to appear in a big way in Sydney. They provided more seats than a contemporary tram, though at the expense of standing capacity.

The first large section of the tramways to close was at Manly. No longer would it be possible to come off the steamer at Manly wharf and pile aboard the Narrabeen tram (first stop Dee Why). The old pleasures were passing, but perhaps there was a new pleasure to be had in riding up the coast on the top deck of one of the new buses.

In the south, another old pleasure was passing away in 1940 with the demise of the last cable trams. After 1937, when the Port Melbourne cable line was replaced by a bus, it seemed that trams in Melbourne might eventually go down the path that had been charted for Sydney. Melbourne was to see its first modern double-deck buses. In view of the war

Crowds boarding the tram at St Kilda Station, 1950. Someone has arranged to fit a pram inside. *(The Age)*

Mrs Irene Stepien aboard No. 774, first car of the day out of South Melbourne Depot, featured in the historic international TV hookup, *Our World*, 26 June 1967. *(Herald and Weekly Times)*

Tram at the Grange. *(D. Jones)*

Afternoon light on the last day of trams in Brisbane.*(D. Jones)*

Tram at King George Square, 1954. Among the decorations for the Royal Visit, 100 trams had patriotic slogans. *(M. Jones)*

An old faithful W2 tram in Victoria Parade, 1976; 48 years in service and as solid as ever. *(C. Jones)*

Z3 at MMTB headquarters. *(C. Jones)*

1041 in the first temporary Bourke Street Mall, 1973. *(C. Jones)*

Rainy evening, Bourke Street. *(MMBW)*

South Melbourne Depot. *(C. Jones)*

Built in 1940, this Auckland tram was withdrawn in 1956 but entered active museum service in 1967. *(C. Jones)*

situation, the cable trams were kept running as long as possible, and even after they had closed the equipment was kept intact in case a cut-off in petrol supplies should require its reopening. Unwilling to see a repeat of the violence which had attended the more recent closures, the Tramways Board arranged for the Bourke Street lines to go quietly. On the Saturday night of 26 October, people went in to the theatres and the cinemas as usual on the tram, but when they came out the trams had gone, and in their place were the shining new green double-deck buses. In many ways it was a sad passing of what Thomas Wood had described almost a decade before as 'the last link with the Australian Middle Ages'.[4] There are nowadays a remarkable number of the old Melbourne cable trams preserved in museum collections, including tramset No.1 of 1885, which gleams resplendent at the Scienceworks Museum at Spotswood, but the first to do anything about it was Alf Twentyman of Northcote. Between 1930 and 1941 he purchased two cars and a dummy, which he installed on their own tracks and with their own shed in his garden. Perhaps a man with a garden full of tram tracks has to spend less time weeding the flower beds, but Alf Twentyman's foresight and enthusiasm, and his great knowledge about the cable cars, were an inspiration to new generations of tram enthusiasts.

Not enjoying the crowded tram, 7 October 1971. *(Herald and Weekly Times)*

The years of the Second World War saw the Australian tramways coping with new difficulties. Through the gloomy night streets the trams rolled, with their lights so dim that conductors had difficulty in deciphering the value of the tickets they were issuing. As the tramwaymen joined the armed forces, their places were often taken by women. Adelaide avoided this by the expedient of coupling many of its

Crowded Prospect tram, 1949. *(The Advertiser)*

Melbourne trams with wartime paint to improve their visibility in the brownout, 1944. *(LaTrobe Library)*

oldest trams to run in pairs, thus effecting a saving in manpower. The 'Bib and Bub' cars, as they were called, developed quite an uncomfortable oscillation at any speed.

The necessity of employing women conductors was forced on Sydney and Melbourne, but it was to be years before prejudices against women driving trams was overcome. It was not until 1976 that, after a three year campaign, women won acceptance from the last Melbourne depot that trams were not too big and heavy to be entrusted to the gentler sex. Joyce Barry was Melbourne's first woman tram driver. She came from the hard life of a farm to be a conductor in 1948 with the idea of saving for a trip overseas. 'Trams became a part of my life. I have seen three generations of children get on the tram and the mothers tell me I used to take them to school.'[5]

In 1956 she began her campaign to be accepted as a driver, surviving all the men's jibes about having to have a sex change with the comment that she didn't think you needed a penis to drive a tram. In changed times, tram driving was 'men's work' no longer. Nowadays the sight of a woman driving a tram brings no comment at all, and passengers are sometimes gratified by the stream of abuse poured by their woman driver upon some recalcitrant motorist needlessly blocking her path. To the morning commuter unfurling his newspaper, it gives a good start to the day to have a smile from the connie with the tram badges on her uniform. Both in the depot and on the road, women have done a great deal for the life on the trams.

The wartime necessity for saving petrol saved some tramlines from early closure, and commonwealth money was made available to build new lines to serve munitions factories in Melbourne, Brisbane, Bendigo and Perth. Overcrowding was endemic, not least because of the tremendous influx of Allied servicemen. Brisbane, with anti-aircraft guns on all its seven hills to meet an enemy who never came, was reluctant host to an army that almost doubled its normal population. Social strains became intense, but the last word must go to Sydney, where an American serviceman noted a change made to a temperance poster inside a tram. 'The World's Greatest Home-Wrecker' it proclaimed, but the last word, 'Drink', had been changed by someone, with feeling, to 'Yanks'.

10

Falling Leaves

One of the great bugbears of all tramway operators was that, not only had they to maintain their tracks, but also the road surface adjacent to them. The great bugbear of the growing tribe of motorists was that the trams stopped in the middle of the road to load and unload their passengers, thus stopping the motorists in their headlong rush to wherever they were going. For a while it seemed that a solution to both problems would be provided by the trolley-bus.

The American term of a 'trackless trolley' came nearer to describing most of the early vehicles of the type. They looked big and boxy, just like the trams, except that they were mounted on bus wheels. This New Testament of transit vehicles could pull into the kerb to load and unload its passengers in safety while allowing other traffic to pass on the outside, and it made use of the public roads without having to contribute to their maintenance, or to the cost of steel rails. Compared to the underpowered motor buses of the day, they could tackle the steepest grades without difficulty, and they were unnervingly quiet. Cyclists in London during the wartime blackout had to take care, not so much of the German bombs, as of the swift, dark, silent, trolley-bus. Trolley-buses were entering service on a minor scale in many places after 1911, but Singapore was one of the first big cities in the world to abandon trams completely for the new vehicle when it made the change at the end of the 1920s. London saw the start of a major trolley-bus conversion in 1931.

William Goodman was the first to experiment with a trolley-bus in Australia, when a single bus was converted for a trial service between Payneham and Paradise. Perth was the first city, in the following year, with a permanent service. The Perth tramways were in a rather depressed state by 1929, without even enough money to buy motors for the newest trams. It was rather a change for the better, then, when on 1 October 1933, three trolley-buses replaced the tram on a route from East Perth to West Leederville. Motor inspector Phil Glover noted: 'At 2.25pm there was an official opening at West Leederville by the Minister for Railways, Mr Willcock. During the afternoon we

Trams and bus at Kings Cross. The scene is the same as picture on p. 52 but the vehicles are more modern. *(postcard)*

Macquarie Street, Hobart. *(postcard)*

Aboard the last tram to North Perth, 1958. *(W.A. Newspapers)*

were not able to cope with the loading and the people were joyriding. Many expressed their appreciation of this new form of travel'.[1]

It was five years before teething troubles, such as the continual dewirements on rough sections of road, had been overcome, but then the tram replacement program began in earnest in the north-western suburbs and on the route beside the Swan to Claremont. University students of that generation remember with great affection the ride in the trolley-bus to the Crawley campus, past the now-vanished curve of Mounts Bay, with its smell of kelp, and the Swan Brewery steaming with promise of libations to come.

Hobart leaned on the Perth experience when it opened its first trolley-bus service in 1935. Alderman Park, who was a great promoter of the system, stated that 'trolley-buses were more flexible than trams, and would be able to maintain a quicker service. Once they had been tried out, he felt sure that trolley-buses would be generally adopted in Hobart'.[2] And so it was. Although the initial routes replaced motor bus services, the trolley-buses were soon starting to displace the trams.

In Adelaide, William Goodman had wished to link the city with Port Adelaide by an interurban tram line the same as the one that was proving so successful to Glenelg, but in this he was defeated by the competing interests of the railway authorities. In its place he opened in 1937 the commencement of what was intended to be a comprehensive trolley-bus system. The first line ran from Light Square to Tussmore, a prestige service where the poles supporting the overhead wires were painted green to match the trees and the conductor was expected to sweep and clean the bus every time it reached the terminus. Unlike Perth and Hobart, Adelaide opted for double-deckers, magnificent in the MTT's livery of Tuscan red and cream. The story is told of the little old lady looking with amazement at the new vehicles and asking what the two poles were for. The crew, with very serious faces, informed her that the poles were to grip onto

Last tram to North Perth, 1958. *(W.A. Newspapers)*

the overhead wires so that the bus would not turn over going around corners. 'Well, fancy that!' said the little old lady.

The trolley-bus service reached Port Adelaide in 1938 to replace the trams, which had been closed a few years earlier. China's loss was Australia's gain during the early war years when a consignment of trolley-bus chassis was diverted from Canton, where it had been intended to build a large system. Canton was now occupied by the Japanese. Twenty-six went to Adelaide, 20 to Hobart and 18 to Perth. These fortuitous arrivals enabled further tram replacements to be contemplated. In Adelaide the new buses, single deckers, were sometimes called 'wombats' because of their low profile and sloped fronts.

The postwar world also seemed to favour trolley-buses. Even the tramway stronghold of Brisbane closed the Edward Street Ferry and Gregory Terrace lines, which required the old-style four-wheel trams, and replaced them with trolley-buses, while in Launceston, William Goodman recommended a wholesale replacement to be undertaken, and so it was. Launceston was the only Australian provincial city so favoured.

For all this, the trolley-bus had a fatal flaw, in that it was electrically powered and limited to its unsightly overhead wires. A transport operator with both motor and trolley-buses would have to keep possibly wasteful duplicate depot and workshop facilities with their specialist staff, for both motor and electric vehicles. Rationalisation always favoured the motor buses and worked against both trolley-buses and trams.

There were other factors also working against the trams. After the tremendous passenger levels of the Second World War, when every vehicle had been made to work hard, whatever state it was in, and when materials badly needed for track reconstruction were required with even more urgency for the war effort, many of the systems were not in a very good shape. Postwar shortages of steel contributed further to their depressed condition and finally, even large tramways began to fail financially.

It was a world where motor cars were rolling off the assembly lines; where people wanted to be rid of the previous restrictions of the crammed discomfort of the peak-hour public transport. More cars; an end to petrol rationing; tram patronage began to sink. Even those who might use the tram for the journey to work would no longer use it for shopping or recreation. The car was available and the era of the suburban shopping centre was at hand. The pioneer development in 1958, in the Brisbane suburb of Chermside, was publicised as 'an island of retailing in a lake of parking'.[3]

In Kalgoorlie, the last Australian tramway owned by a private company, the Kalgoorlie Electric Tramways Ltd, passed into public ownership under the

P-class tram. *(LaTrobe Library)*

Sydney trams in the rain, Castlereagh Street, 1949. *(National Library)*

Eastern Goldfields Transport Board in 1949. Patronage had fallen away badly and the new owner was able to close the tramway down with only minimal bus replacement in 1952. In their later years there had been some freak accidents in Kalgoorlie, including two trams badly damaged when struck by lightning at the same place on the same day in 1947, and another tram demolished when it was hit by a train on a level crossing the following year.

A major change was in the wind in Adelaide following the retirement in 1950, at the age of 78, of the great tramwayman, William Goodman. He left the empire which he had created to Charles Moyes, who remained as general manager for less than two years. It was a crucial period, as the Municipal Tramways Trust was on the verge of major expansion, with new tram and trolley-bus lines under construction, and a new class of tram almost ready to take the road. At the same time it was revealed that its financial reserves were exhausted and its deficits would become the responsibility of the municipalities represented on the Trust. Typically of the time, a firm of American consultants recommended the scrapping of the trams and the conversion of the whole system to one-man bus operation. The government guaranteed finance for the conversion. Thus only one new tram was completed and the second was cut up for scrap. The trolley-buses that had been intended to open up new territory for electric vehicles were made to replace some of the trams, and one by one the lines began to close. By 1958 only the Glenelg line was left. The consultants had admitted that this was 'the finest transit service operated by the Trust',[4] while still condemning it to bus conversion. Somehow, perhaps by the creation of the fiction that the line was really a railway, and so not to be included in the events that were overtaking the tramways, closure never came. Even when the last trolley-bus departed, 'unwept, unhonoured and unsung', in 1963, the Glenelg trams soldiered on. They still do today.

Supported by the highest relative fares in Australia, the Hobart Municipal Tramways had been relatively secure. Nevertheless, the decrepitude of some of the track on the Sandy Bay line was responsible for the overturning of two double-deck trams in 1946 and, rather than relay the track, all the double deckers were cut down and the fleet soon became standardised with modern bogie saloon cars. Then there came the disastrous slide in patronage of the mid-1950s which caused a government takeover of the trams and trolley-buses and a significant lowering of the fares. For a brief moment people stayed with public transport, but its impoverished condition left little solution but the universal panacea of motor-bus replacement. The eight

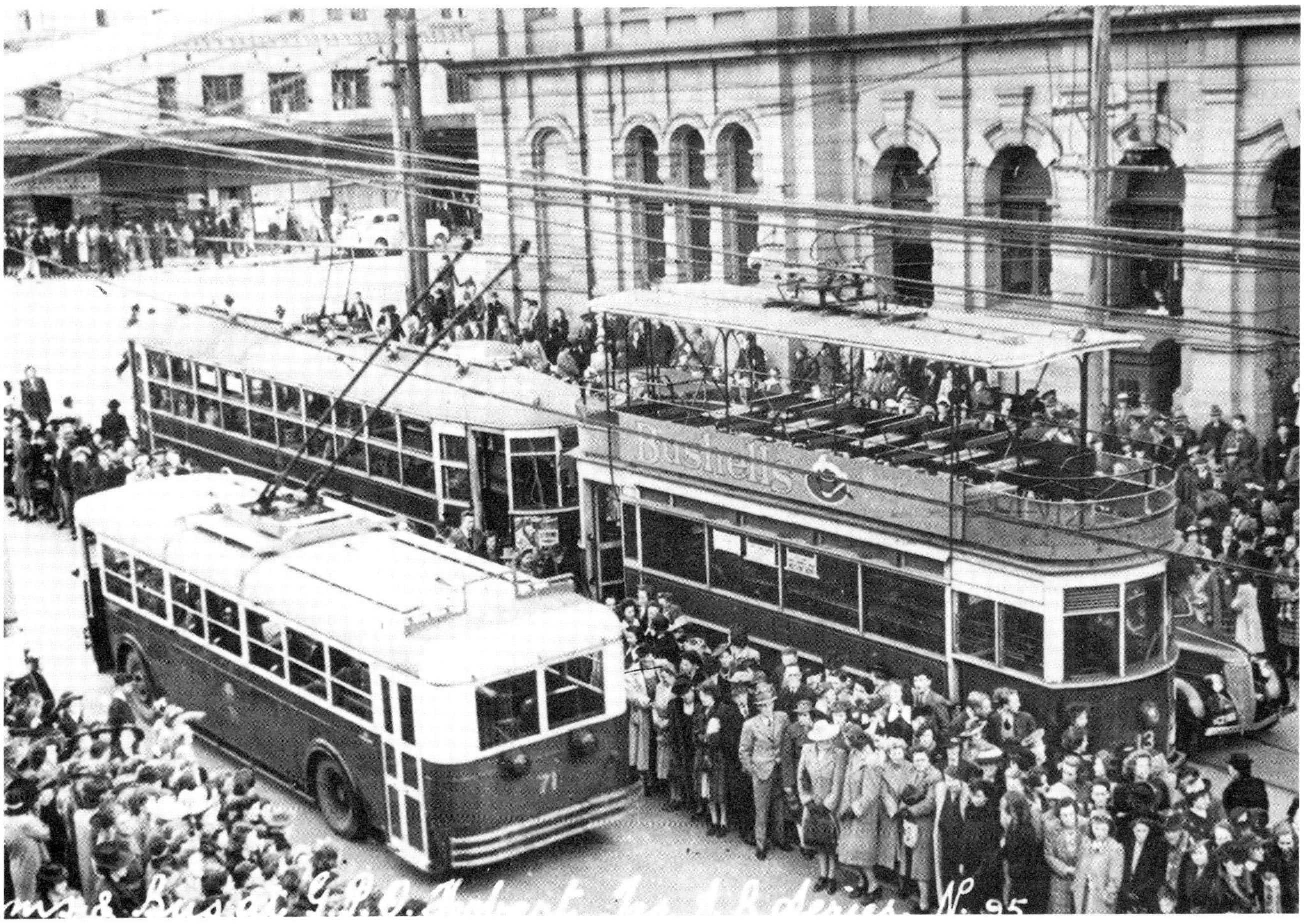

Trams and trolley-bus, Hobart. *(TTMS)*

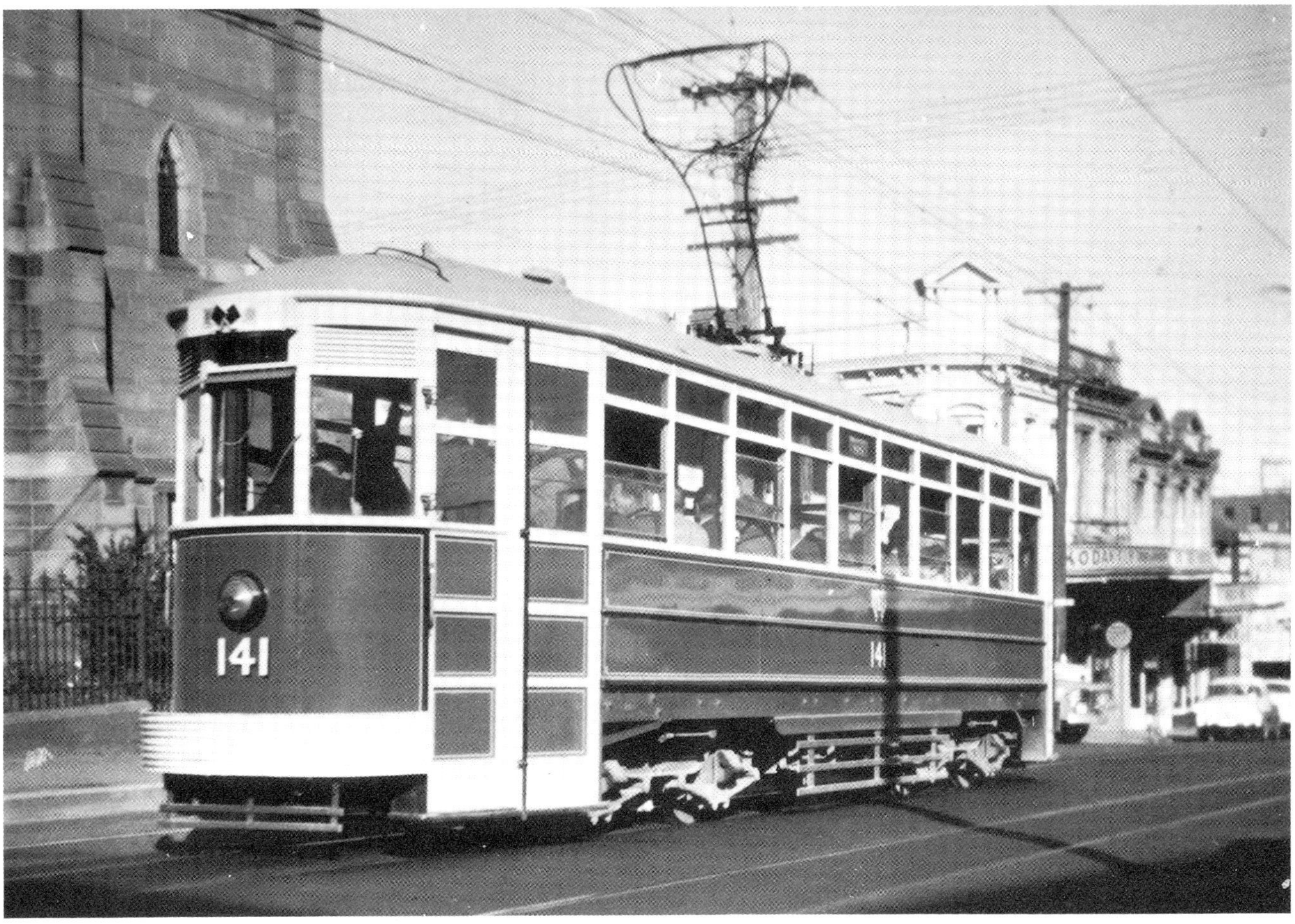

Modern Hobart tram; built in 1952, it was the only tram to be preserved when the system closed in 1960. *(I. Cooper)*

A Hobart tram overturned, 1946. *(Mercury)*

Adelaide's only modern tram, the H1-class car entered service early in 1953. Thirty-nine others were never built. *(STA)*

kilometre route to Glenorchy provided a third of all the revenue on the Hobart tram and bus system. Even in 1960 when, as the last tramline in Tasmania, it closed, it was still run by trams with an average age of only 17 years (not old in the life of a tram). It could have been run almost indefinitely. Crippled by the power rationing following the drought of 1967, when in that year's terrible bushfires trolley-bus No.234 was gutted in the suburban street at Cascades, the trolley-buses were soon to follow the trams into oblivion.

The longest drawn-out agony was reserved for the great Sydney tramway system which, even in 1948, was the largest in Australia. Faced with the necessity of investment on a huge scale to remedy the neglect of war, and with the operations of the trams descending once more into the red, the McKell Government announced in 1946 a complete conversion to buses by 1961. Even this would require a thousand new buses and costs of the order of £3 million. That the issue was very much alive was illustrated by the pledge of the new premier, James McGirr, in his 1947 policy speech, to build 500 new trams for Sydney. The cost, however, was such that the government paused, uncertain how to proceed. At the same time a scathing report from the auditor-general condemned the financial plight of the operation, the general antiquity of its vehicles, the decrepitude of the track and hesitation in placing new orders. A rise in fares matched a rise in staff wages. In desperation the government looked for a report on possible solutions from the best authorities available. William Goodman had declined the task, but two senior and experienced men from Hobart and Melbourne were able to present a report late in 1947. The gist of the report was that the trams in Newcastle and Ashfield should be replaced immediately by buses, while the 500 new saloon trams should be built so that fare evasion, which had become epidemic on the crossbench cars, could be contained.

Orders for the first 250 new trams were placed in mid-1948, though the price was higher than that of the equivalent vehicles in Melbourne and Brisbane, and the design was a conservative repeat of that of the early 1930s.

Then came another experts' report, this time from some London consultants. Typically of advice from a city where the trams were being firmly phased out as a matter of government policy, the report urged that the new tram program be stopped immediately and that all lines should be closed by 1960.[5] So far was this out of step with the wishes of the people of Sydney that the closure of the Watsons Bay tramway in late 1949 was followed by protests sufficiently vigorous to have it reopened in the middle of the following year.

Hobart's first trolley-bus, 1935. The first Hobart and Perth trolley-buses were virtually identical. *(Tasmanian Library)*

Indeed, the Watsons Bay tramway was the busiest in Australia, with a tram every 40 seconds out of the city in the evening peak on 1948 schedules, and an average of 50 000 passengers a day.

For a brief period it seemed that the trams could be saved.

As ever, money was the problem. The cost of the new trams turned out to be half as high again as had been estimated, and a lot higher than contemporary Brisbane trams, which were exhibiting many superior features. Production had been slow to get under way, but it was not slow to have stopped. The hundredth tram of the brave new plan for 500, car No.2087, was the last.

The cause of the trams was not helped by two spectacular accidents which befell corridor trams in 1952. No.1890 began slipping on wet leaves on the track by Taronga Park Zoo and rapidly got out of control. At almost 100 kilometres per hour it hurtled down the track towards the ferry wharf, through the fence at the end and into the Harbour. From there it was forlornly rescued by the floating crane. The tram which must take the world record for the shortest ever service life was No.2018. On the very day it was first placed in service it was in collision with a truck at Petersham. The explosion of the truck's petrol tank deluged both vehicles in flames and what was left of the tram was taken away for scrap.

Sadly for the trams and for the people, operating deficits continued to rise. Something had to be done, and that something was ushered in by a new transport minister late in 1953. The trams were to go. The anti-tram lobby could point to the rapidly increasing traffic congestion; to pictures of trams stranded in a sea of fuming motor vehicles; to the constant delays and late running; and to yet another consultants' report. The experts this time came from New York, where the last trams had vanished five years before. Their report, released in 1957, urged the conversion of all trams and buses to one-man operation as the only solution to the transport deficit.

To support the vain theory that buses could reverse the transport deficit and alleviate traffic congestion, the trams were swept away like autumn leaves in the wind. The rattle of the wheels on crossings, the hum of the motors, the pump and hiss of the air brakes and the kiss of the trolley wheel on the overhead wires were heard no more. The trams departed with wreaths and tears, for who would welcome a bus with bands, flags and speeches? The most picturesque of all tram depots, at Fort Macquarie, with its towers and crenellations an echo of Francis Greenway's old fort on the site, closed in 1955. Do present day visitors to Sydney's Opera House ever hear the ghostly echoes in its basements of the rumble of tram wheels, or the even fainter bark of a 24-pounder cannon?

Perth trolley-bus in Wellington Street, 1933. *(W.A. Government Printer)*

Enthusiasts riding the rails in the oldest tram they can find prior to the closure of the Pitt and Castlereagh Street lines, 1957. *(C. Jones collection)*

On a dark September night in 1957 the last tram for Dulwich Hill encountered, of all things, an altar built across the tracks in City Road. Here the theological students from Moore College were ready in their robes to perform a brief funeral service before allowing it to proceed to the strains of 'Auld Lang Syne'.

On the Sydney Harbour Bridge, the closure of the North Sydney tramways allowed two more lanes to be given over from the trams to the victorious motorists. Regular commuters could regret the bright trams in their underground station, and the fast journey across the bridge, as the replacing buses battled their way centimetre by centimetre in the heavy evening traffic up to the toll gates. So they all went. On the last day of tramway operation in Sydney, 25 February 1961, there were crowds out everywhere along the lines to Maroubra and La Perouse to see the show. To avoid vandalism, the closure was to take place in the mid afternoon instead of at night, and all day the trams were swamped with joyriders. Cameras clicked all along the line.

Sydney has regretted the loss of its trams, to such an extent that in 1974 a major study was undertaken to consider their reintroduction. Despite this, and subsequent proposals, time, like an ever-running stream, has so far not brought them back again. But for just a moment, prior to the opening of the Eastern Suburbs Railway, an old track scrubber was brought back from the museum of trams to prepare the tracks for the trains. To anyone seeing it down in the dim tunnels, it would have seemed like a ghost from the past.

11

Farewell Brisbane Ladies

'I feel that if we have to make a choice between public and private transport into the city, we must give priority to public transport which carries the greater number of people. In short, our policy is people before vehicles.'[1]

With these admirable sentiments, Alderman Wilfred Coutts, chairman of the transport committee of the Brisbane City Council, announced in November 1952 a 25 year transport plan for the city. Although the plan was mainly one of policy, without many specific projects, it message was clear in the newspaper headlines which greeted it: 'Council Decides to Keep Trams as Best Service for Public.'[2]

The plan was, in fact, the testament to the city of its great tramwayman, Sydney Quinn, who was due to retire the next month at the age of 65. In 1948 Quinn had travelled to North America, Britain and Europe to study the latest trends in city transport and he immediately began to introduce modern features such as resilient wheels, roller bearings and helical gears into the latest trams. Brisbane could feel with pride that it had some of the best trams in Australia. Had it not been for strict exchange controls and import restrictions, he might have joined with his protégé Robert Risson, newly elevated as chairman of the Melbourne and Metropolitan Tramways Board, in introducing the revolutionary American PCC trams to the two cities.[3] As it was, the Brisbane trams were bright and smart, with fluorescent lights and big convex mirrors at each end of the saloon above the door to the motorman's cabin so the conductor could check whether the doors were clear.

The story is told, in illustration of how good the trams were, that a motorist was pulled over late at night by the police for speeding. He complained that he would not have been so unhappy at the event if the tram had not been going even faster.

In 1953 Alderman Coutts was able to announce to

Welcoming lights of a tram at the Grange at night. *(D. Campbell)*

the beleaguered New South Wales transport minister, with pure insular chauvinism, that Brisbane already led Australia and possibly the world in tramway transport.

At this time there were moves in Sydney to borrow a complete Brisbane tram for tests with a view to possibly introducing the design there. Brisbane, unlike most other cities, had pushed ahead with tramway extensions. The new line to Chermside ran in its own reservation between gardens of roses, to everyone's delight and pride. The last extension, opened in the usual way with flags and crowds, saw the trams reach Mount Gravatt in 1951. Next in line had it not been for shortages of steel and loan money would have been an extension of the Cavendish Road line, and another from Stafford to Everton Park. New trams continued to emerge from the Milton workshops at regular intervals up to 1955, slowly replacing old vehicles. The shortage of money stopped the next three until 1959. Other factors working towards a long life for the tramways were the high standard of vehicle maintenance and the fact that most of the track was strongly laid in mass concrete. During the 1950s the trolley-bus system was built up, replacing motor buses for the most part, but also one tram branch line. Ironically, there were never enough trolley-buses in the fleet to maintain full services on the lines that were built. The fleet in 1960 was no fewer than 25 trolley-buses short.

AEC Regal Bus at Mount Coottha. A bus route could be infinitely extended. *(postcard)*

Still, service frequencies in Brisbane were the best in the nation, and it was the boast of Allan and Stark's department store in the city that every tram ran past its doors.

One oddity demonstrated the difference. At a couple of places around Woolloongabba, the sleek streamlined tram would sometimes have to stop for the puffing of an antique steam train as it crossed the streets for access to the local rail yards. The train, of course, had to be accompanied by a man walking in front with a flag and a bell.

The fiveways at Woolloongabba, with tram, train and trolley-bus. The tram signal box is at the left. The train has been preceded by a man with a bell and a red flag. *(D. Campbell)*

Firemen still working at Paddington Depot the morning after, 30 September 1962. *(C. Jones collection)*

At the end of the 1950s, after a controversial report by W. D. Scott & Co, feelers were put out to the state government to take over the tramways from the city council. The answer was a definite No.

In common with every other city, Brisbane saw people turning away from public transport to the private car and televised recreation, with the consequent loss of profitability for the transport operator, but the Brisbane tramways were under no real threat until the election as lord mayor in 1961 of Clem Jones.[4] Jones was a Labor man of the old school; 43 years old when elected, he kept an iron grip on the city for a record term, to the extent that the city was seen as a major source of opposition power and patronage by the conservative, rural-oriented state government. It was a major tenet of his ideology that every person should have the right to drive their cars into the city for whatever purpose, and if public transport got in the way, so much the worse. In an interview ten years later he stated categorically:

> We are trying to get rid of public transport.
>
> I'm not an anti-motor car man. There are two things I believe people are entitled to: a home and a motor car. What's the good of having a society which provides for a man to own a car and tells him he must leave it at home five days a week?
>
> I believe our job is to appreciate this age of the motor car.[5]

Although the Brisbane tramways were highly efficient, comparing well in matters of cost with Melbourne, the department no longer had the strong hand of Sydney Quinn at the head of its administration and it became vulnerable to the political winds of the time, even to the sacking of one of its general managers.

The first Phoenix-class car entered service on 24 September 1963. *(BCC)*

In particular the demise of the Sydney tramways seemed, to many people, to leave Brisbane clinging to a piece of the outmoded past. Typically of the loss of confidence which the undertaking was experiencing was the feeling of the tramway men that their uniforms should be overhauled. They felt embarrassed when tourists asked them to pose in front of their trams in their traditional 'foreign legion' caps. The caps went in 1961, though the inspectors retained theirs, perhaps because their colour and braiding made them look sufficiently like French generals.

Then in 1962 there came a great disaster. The Paddington car shed was one of the three big depots that served Brisbane. It was a great rambling wooden building, built on a steep site so that its rear end was supported on tall wooden stumps 15 metres above the ground. Its scheduled replacement by a new depot at Milton had never gone ahead. At 7.30 p.m. on 29 September a resident of a house situated in the very shadow of the depot's bulk saw sparks falling under the floor in the vicinity of the oil storeroom. The depot master, notified immediately, called the local Ithaca Fire Brigade. Water pressure was low and the firemen had difficulty locating the seat of the fire. Quite suddenly it flared up, spreading along the inspection pits. The few men on hand managed to drive out only three trams into the street and save the cash boxes before the depot became an inferno of flame. By the

No. 473 posed, 1949. *(BTMS)*

time five more fire engines arrived, the most that could be done was to concentrate on saving the adjacent houses and shops while the depot, filled with the burning shells of 65 trams, blazed high in the night sky.

It was reckoned that the losses amounted to £300 000 in trams and £200 000 in the building, and that, with the cost of a new tram at £12 000, replacement would mean expenditure of the order of £1 500 000.

The resulting acute shortage of trams for peak services was met initially by bringing out all the old warriors up to 50 years old from their semi-retirement

Trams in depot. *(D. Campbell, courtesy BTMS)*

Trams in Queen Street, Brisbane. (*D. Campbell*)

in the back corners of the other depots, and by importing 15 inadequate buses up the road in a convoy from Sydney. A rather more final solution was imposed in the quiet of Christmas Day, when the Bulimba Ferry, Kalinga, Rainworth and Toowong lines were closed. Public protest, mobilised at the end of the holiday period, was ignored.

Even then a strong administration could have saved the trams. In 1963 money was made available to construct eight more trams, making extensive use of parts already on hand or salvaged from Paddington. The new cars were known as the Phoenix class, as having, like the bird of legend, risen from the ashes of the great fire. Tram No.554, which rolled out of Milton shops in March 1964, was to remain for the whole of its working life, the newest tram in Australia. Consultants in 1962 recommended the integration of city transport, and Alderman Harvey, chairman of the transport committee, and others at council level, were still supporters of the trams.

Brisbane at this time was involved with some major projects, as a result of the firm administration of Clem Jones and his town clerk, James Slaughter. For the first time, there would be a town plan. The huge sewerage scheme, as well as the bringing of the roads up to standard, was absorbing substantial finance. In

Tram beside the river at Hamilton. (*postcard*)

1963 also, the council handed over its power stations to the state government, thus losing control of pricing policy.

Apart from the general antipathy to trams which was growing in the council, there were the hard figures of passenger decline and the way that, from 1960 onwards, costs began significantly to outstrip revenue. Slaughter was adamant that the solution was the

A city-bound tram speeds along St Kilda Road, 1971. *(C. Jones)*

By the Arts Centre, Moomba time, 1977. *(C. Jones)*

Hong Kong tram, 1982. *(C. Jones)*

This Christchurch tram ran in service from 1922 to 1953, and again at Ferrymead Park museum from 1970. *(C. Jones)*

Wellington trams in museum. *(C. Jones)*

Old-style Bangkok tram on the Bangsue line, 1959. *(W. Higgins)*

Riding in a museum tram, 1980. *(D. Robertson)*

Modernised Bangkok tram at Wat Bowonniwet, 1959. *(W. Higgins)*

Although clearly stating that it is 'Not Carrying Passengers', this special tour tram is well filled. *(C. Jones)*

Hong Kong trams, 1971. *(D. Jones)*

Tram at Middle Park. *(C. Jones)*

Drop-centre tram. *(D. Campbell)*

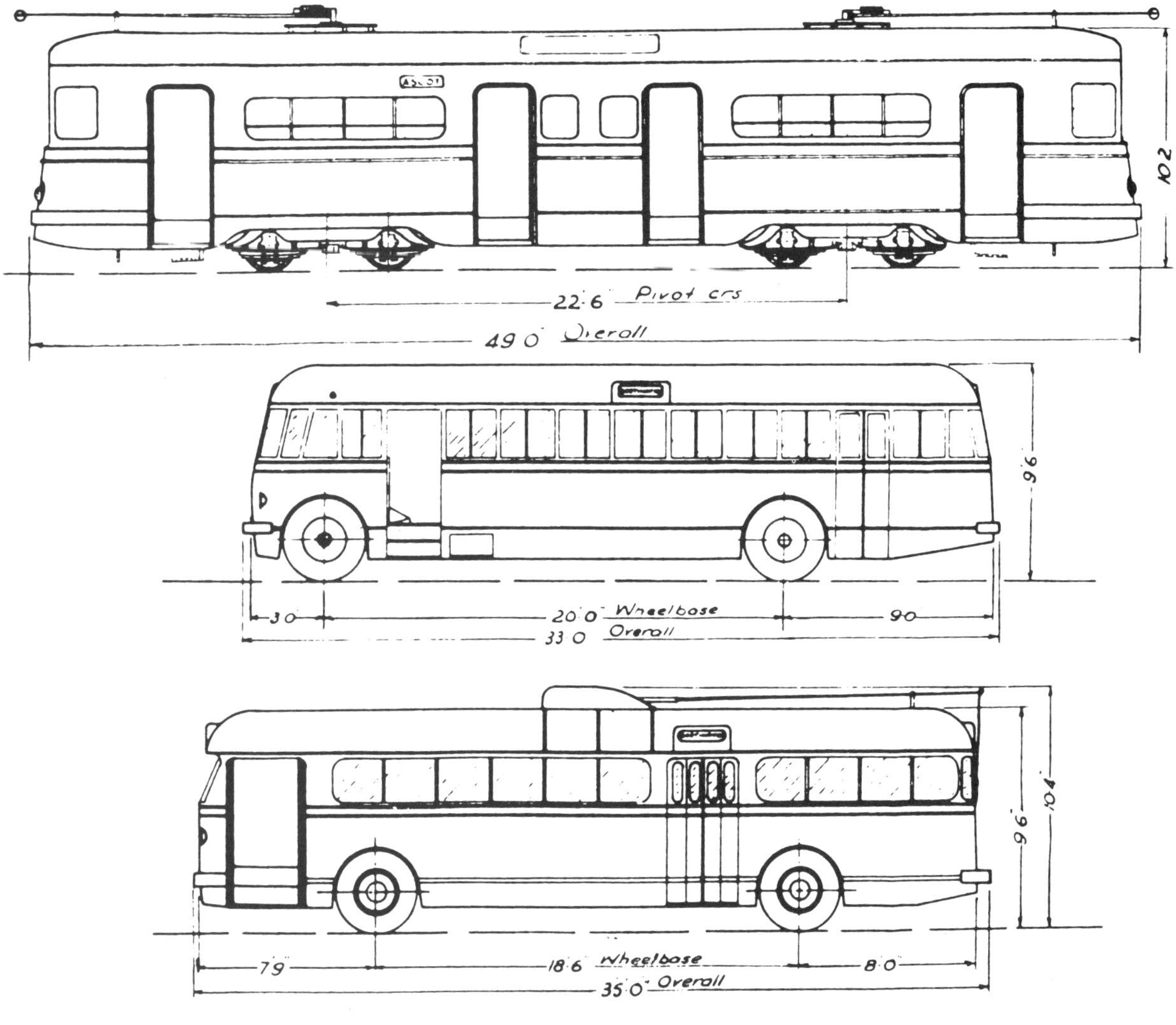

Tram, bus and trolley bus plan. *(C. Jones collection)*

Tram at Mount Gravatt. This important southern terminus should have seen an eventual 2.8-kilometre extension to Garden City. *(National Library)*

wholesale introduction of one-man buses. Furthermore, between 1963 and 1973 the Brisbane City Council's vehicles lost one in every two of their passengers. That this result was far worse than that experienced in Melbourne can, in retrospect, be firmly attributed to the destruction of the tramways. The preference of people for railed transport may be seen in the substantial increases in patronage enjoyed by the Brisbane suburban railways at the same time that the trams were being phased out. It was a wanton and unnecessary act.

Ominously, the consultants were called in, in this case the American Wilbur Smith and Associates, to undertake a road traffic and transport study. The result was a grandiose plan typical of the 1960s, proposing a massive system of urban freeways, with no fewer than three new bridges in the city area and another on the lower river. The world would be made perfect for the private motorist at a cost of £178 000 000. Two suburban rail lines were to be closed and, of course, the whole tram and trolley bus system had to be scrapped. As this accorded well with the council's wishes, the trams had all gone before the first section of freeway was opened in 1973. The last irony was that, following great public discontent, the same consultants were later called upon to provide a plan for public transport. Their 1971 plan mutely acknowledged the vanished trams by its provision for an elaborate series of electric underground railways.

Moves against the trams proceeded under a cloak of secrecy as the old trams were scrapped and new bus orders increased. The completion of a new big bus depot at Toowong and the advancing work on the new Victoria Bridge determined the council's timetable. In mid-1968 Clem Jones announced that all tram and trolley-bus routes would be abandoned within the coming financial year. The decision had already been taken two years before, when express buses were put into competition with the trams on the main routes. It was to be one of the swiftest changeovers from a large tramway to buses ever attempted. The Grange and Ashgrove routes closed in August. Public protest was to no avail. 'SAVE THE TRAMS', read the posters, 'Don't let the wreckers stop this multi-million dollar transport system'. The last day of trams in Brisbane was Sunday 13 April 1969. Crowds of people were everywhere, with cameras and not a few 'foreign legion' caps. The trams ran to capacity all day.

So passed the trams, sadly mourned by the people and replaced by the unloved buses. Brisbane without them has become another city. The few surviving tramcars, lovingly tended by the Brisbane Tramway Museum Society, are exiled to their outer suburban site where they can no longer disturb the rights of the private motorist. Their tracks still support the bitumen of many main roads. It is not just nostalgia which leads many Brisbane people to say that they should never have gone.

12

Trams are Here to Stay

To a visitor such as Thomas Wood, who saw Australia during the Great Depression, Melbourne seemed a city characterised by its trams. 'Those trams! Giants, green and white, charging through miles of lighted streets. They find their way to suburbs so big and so far away that in time you are ready to believe the entire population of Victoria lives in Greater Melbourne and works in its factories.'[1]

By 1950 Melbourne's tramway system stood as the largest in Australia. In the troubled postwar era it was fortunate to gain a strong administrator in Robert Risson. In 1949 Hector Bell retired as chairman of the Melbourne and Metropolitan Tramways Board at the age of 72. His career in tramways dated back to some of the earliest electric lines in Melbourne, and he had sat on the board as the new metropolitan electric system was built. To replace him, the 48 year old Risson was lured from his position near to the centre of power of the Brisbane Tramways. He had emerged from the war as a major general in the Australian Engineers, an appropriate rank, as he was to hold the Melbourne tramways firm during a long siege while every other stronghold, even Brisbane, fell. His first battle was in the organisation itself.

Melbourne was badly affected by the coal strike in July and August 1949. At one stage a destroyer was brought alongside a collier in the Yarra so that her men could unload the coal necessary to keep the city's gas supply from failing. Power cuts had meant reduced services and terrible overcrowding of the trams that were on the road, while other staff had to be stood down. Inflation was beginning to take its toll of money values. With these events as a recent background, the Tramway and Motor Omnibus Employees Association requested a £1 per week rise over the 1949 award. It was rejected. The union was ready for a trial of strength and after all the trams had returned to their depots on 22 February 1950, the men were on strike. No accommodation was forthcoming on either side, so Risson sought, and was granted, the deregistration of the union in the middle of March. Melbourne was without its trams, the streets jammed with cars for 60 days. When, as a result of some concessions being offered, the men returned to work, 400 of them had departed permanently into other jobs.

Part of the equipment for Risson's battle for the tramways emerged on the street in mid-1950 in the form of tram No.980, Australia's first PCC tram. This advance in tramcar technology had been the result of the reversal of fortunes which had been experienced by American tramway operators during the 1920s with the rise of the motor car. The Electric Railway Presidents' Conference Committee had been formed in 1931 to finance research into the tram of the future, whose superior qualities would redeem the fortunes of the operators. The first of the new type, named for the initials of the committee, a PCC car, emerged in 1934, and the type remained in production in the USA until the early 1950s. Melbourne, as the most advanced of the Australian tramway systems, had been interested in importing a PCC car for trials in 1938, but the Australian Customs had refused to waive crippling import duties. After the war the project continued to hang fire because of the dollar shortage. Finally a set of trucks and control equipment was purchased and installed in a conventional tram body. Financial constraints prevented further cars of the type being built, but features such as resilient wheels were incorporated in later trams. Up to 1956, new trams were being built for Melbourne at a rate of about 14 a year.

Another important section of Risson's defence of the tramways was the improvements which were gradually introduced for traffic management, and for separating tram and car traffic. The first 'prow' type safety zones were an early example of this, in 1953.

A major victory was the building of the Bourke Street tramway. For 15 years the cable tracks had sat unused in the street while the buses squealed to their stops and people queued to get aboard. Even when the buses were new the people did not like them. As a result, the construction of a tramway was listed as an 'A' priority by the co-ordinator of works at the end of the war. The scheme was set back by the premier, Thomas Hollway, who, returning in 1949 from a trip overseas where he had noticed a certain amount of tramway abandonment, called for an urgent report by the minister for public works. The Tramways Board made sure its report was a winner. It compared the relative merits of trolley buses, diesel buses and trams and came to the conclusion that, given the already extensive tramway system of which the lines would be an integral part, buses would be both less efficient and more expensive. A census of passengers on the route showed 'an overwhelming majority in favour of trams', and every municipality involved expressed a 'preference for trams'.

The government, presented with a very strong defence, after mature consideration gave it their blessing. The actual start was delayed by shortages of materials, labour and loan money until after the Queen's visit in 1954, but after that, everything progressed at a good pace. By the time the whole scheme was completed in 1956, more than 14 kilometres of new tram route had been added to the Melbourne system, a marvel for such a late date, and the last new construction Melbourne was to see for many years. *The Argus* reported that:

> Traffic never flowed more smoothly in Melbourne's infamous rush hour than it did in this new tram street yesterday.
>
> Being a veteran of five bumpy years experience on the double decker buses I can vouch for the improved comfort of the trams.
>
> There's no ear piercing scream of brakes, no sudden lurching stops, no jumping for safety as the bus swings to the kerb.[2]

Unfortunately, lack of finance forced the abrupt cutting-off of the new tram construction program at this point.

If there were victories, there were also defeats. The Victorian Railways had become disenchanted with their role as the operator of two electric street railways, and after the end of the war they were seeking to divest themselves of the responsibility. Initially, public pressure demanded that the trams be retained. The first closures were staved off for ten years while investigations proceeded about what should be done. The Tramways Board could not afford the cost of taking them over and nor would the government finance their rehabilitation. Slowly they became rough, run-down and shabby, a progression which led, as in other places, to their eventual closure between 1955 and 1959. On the main system there were services to be withdrawn and economies to be made, such as the closure of the all-night tram services, and eventually the closure of all lines that required to be worked by the small four-wheel trams. This process culminated in the replacement by buses of all the local Footscray lines, and their depot, so often recently the scene of industrial action, being turned over to buses in 1962.

A number of different city plans over the years have reluctantly admitted the existence and likely continuance of the tramway system. The MMTB, however, was able to draw on its own planning resources both to consider future developments and to combat attacks from any fuzzy-minded idealists who might propose that the city could one day do without the rails in the streets. As the European tramways blossomed in the modern environment, there were eyes in Melbourne that noted all the new developments and how, in a day of less austerity, they could be applied here. In 1962 the board had designed a scheme for underground tramlines in the centre of Melbourne, and was urging that the work should be undertaken as soon as the underground railway was complete.[3] Swanston Street, where there was a tram every 80 seconds in normal times, and in peak periods a continual stream, seemed to be a good candidate as the first underground line after the German style. To show just how things could be done, the replacement of the awkward bottleneck of St Kilda Junction by a new road system in 1968 involved diverting one of the tramlines under the street and onto its own reservation in the centre of a short section of traffic freeway. Even while the big projects flagged, Robert Risson was strengthening the defences of his tramways; duplicating the last sections of single track, relaying old tracks in mass concrete, making sure that vehicles were well lit and stops well marked. Even the simple matter of paintwork helped. Never did the Melbourne trams fall to the shabby appearance which had been so often seen in Sydney. The Melbourne trams looked as though someone cared.

All of this was, perhaps, vitally important, as the anti-tram pro-motor lobby was never far away and people were turning away from the trams and using more and more their private vehicles. Between 1957 and 1972, tram patronage was halved. After 1956 people began to turn to television for their recreation. The cinemas began to close and the evening trams ran with fewer and fewer passengers. Strikes did not help either, for every time the trams were out some people turned to their cars and never came back. The inevitably rising costs of the system would bring in their wake a rise in fares and, almost as night follows day, fewer people would travel. Then, ominously, by the late 1960s it was becoming plain that the tramways would never again return a profit. In fortunate ignorance of the great leap of inflation to come, the board in 1970 found itself losing one cent on the average 15-cent fare paid by every passenger.

To a great extent it was the times that were against the trams, and for all the defences, both physical and corporate, with which Robert Risson had hedged them, he knew that two things were needed if the battle was at last to be won. He needed new tramlines and he needed new trams. In 1963 he toured Europe and saw what he wanted. Gliding silently through the streets of continental Europe were a new generation of trams, smartly and efficiently carrying off their loads of

Dandenong Road. The contrast in streetscape with the picture on page 63 is striking. *(C. Jones)*

Balaclava Junction, with the heavy web of wires for the 'Grand Union'. *(C. Jones)*

passengers in their great cities. No longer could critics sustain an argument that Melbourne was behind the times in retaining its trams. The tram and nothing else, especially in the broad straight streets of Melbourne, was the vehicle of the future.

Although 100 new trams were considered a necessity, they were not to be obtained easily. On the general style of the most recent trams built for Goteborg in Sweden, a detailed design was prepared, full-scale mock-ups erected, and eventually work on a prototype was set in hand. For this, the existing PCC car was sacrificed and its equipment, along with various other gear — some from Germany, some even from a museum trolley bus in Hobart — installed in

Collins Street. *(C. Jones)*

a new body. The new tram, No.1041, rolled out onto the tracks for trials in 1973, resplendent in orange and green. Unfortunately its entry into service appears to have been a little hurried as, on an official first run with a number of politicians (who always like to create a good impression), it broke down and the politicians had to walk the rest of the way. The new tram saw the battle won, however, as an order was placed for 100 of a similar design. Melbourne would have its new trams, 10 years late maybe, but at least it would have them. The Z class and their successors, with their European technology, represent the modern age of tramways in Australia.

Designed as they were to minimise fare evasion, and with a rate of acceleration more than double that of the older trams, the new vehicles generated some differences of opinion among the travelling public. The MMTB, in fact, recognised the nostalgia that had grown around trams by instituting heritage services with its oldest vehicles. Even an old crossbench car of 1906 was brought back from its unromantic semi-retirement as a freight car and reconverted to its original splendour.

The other battle that required to be fought and won was that of new tramway extensions. Although the suburbs expanded endlessly, no actual extension of the perimeter of the tramway system had been built since the war. The board's first moves came in 1967 when the government rejected its proposal for a one-kilometre extension of the East Preston line towards LaTrobe University. It was not until the latter part of the 1970s that public and government opinion coincided to the extent that a new extension could be built. This was for no less than 3.5 kilometres, from Burwood to East Burwood. The new tramway was a showpiece, enabling the new trams to kick up their heels as they sped along the reservation in the centre of the highway. Its success led to approval being given at last for the new line to LaTrobe University and Bundoora. As the tramway recruiting posters had it, 'Trams are here to stay'.

During 1978 the Ministry of the Arts began to sponsor the painting, in a pop art style, of several of the older trams. One of them, the project of the noted artist Clifton Pugh, featured birds, butterflies, etc. 'Then I found the route was to be through Collingwood and Hawthorn football territory, and one cannot be one-eyed in that world, so there is a magpie and a hawk on each side!'[4] During the course of the work a window was stolen with some painted butterflies on it. Although the artist disclaimed it, someone, somewhere, has a potentially valuable work of art, and certainly a unique one — tram window by Clifton Pugh.[5]

Despite the huge deficits caused by the inflation of the 1970s and despite the negative findings of the 1980 Loney report; Robert Risson's successors have carried their tramway triumphantly into the modern age.[6] Tram patronage no longer falls, as the people of Melbourne realise again what they have probably always known, that the tram is the faithful servant of the city, knitting together the urban fabric, friendly and dependable. The tram is justly the symbol of Melbourne, the largest tramway system in the English-speaking world.[7]

Major General Risson prepared to lead his troops, after his return from a trip to study tramways overseas, 1963. *(MMTB)*

13

Trams International

Just as in Australia there was once scarcely a city worthy of the name that did not have its own tramway, so it was in the rest of the world. The power to survive was not given to them all. In America, where once trams were numbered in their tens of thousands, the all-conquering automobile, by fair means or foul, swept most of them away. Yet in a handful of the better cities, places such as Boston and San Francisco, the tram has never died, and in others they are starting to come back. Seattle even imported some Melbourne trams to start a new service after a gap of over 40 years.[1] Closer to home, there is still a large tramway system in India at Calcutta; Japan has a number of tramways, notably at Hiroshima; and Hong Kong retains the last tramway in the world to be fully equipped with British-style double-deck trams. Japan now even exports new trams to the United States, where once the industry was the foremost in the world.

New Zealand, so close to Australia in many ways, had a number of tramways and did not usher out its last tram until 1964. In fact, as the last streamer-decked trams in New Zealand proceeded in sad procession through the crowded streets of Wellington on 2 May 1964, Councillor Manthel, chairman of the city's transport committee, voiced an almost universal feeling that 'if Wellington had been blessed with wide streets the trams might well have been saved'.[2] As it is, the New Zealand capital is the last city in that country to retain trolley buses, and the only one to have an electric suburban railway.

The first tram in New Zealand was on a short line in Nelson in 1862. Obviously unsure of what sort of an animal it was, they called it a 'bus'.

Wellington started with steam trams in 1878 and the new form of transport soon spread to Dunedin and Christchurch. In its tramway experience, New Zealand was much more like Great Britain than was Australia, as the steam trams soon fell into disfavour and were largely replaced by horses. Only on the broad flat streets of Christchurch were the steam trams retained, the little English motors pulling their long strings of trailers out of Cathedral Square and off to the suburbs, or perhaps for an excursion to the beach. Invercargill,

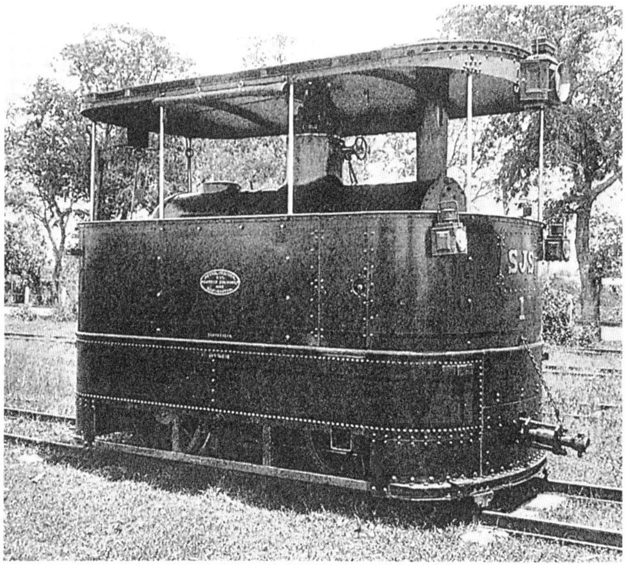

Samarang Joana 13-ton loco. *(Gedenkboek)*

prosperous in the wake of the gold rushes, boasted the southernmost tramway in the world, and in fact all three of the tramways in the South Island of New Zealand lay nearer the pole than those in either Tasmania or Chile. The big city, Auckland, commenced with horse trams in 1884. Here the unfortunate beasts had to contend with some quite steep gradients, up to 1 in 12. To tackle these a heavy draughthorse would be hitched up to the front to help the two lighter tram horses, and even then in the evening peak hour the passengers would sometimes have to jump off and jam road metal under the wheels as the overloaded tram dragged its team backwards down the hill. It was always a hard life for a horse, working on the trams.

Subsequently, Auckland had the steepest electric tramway in New Zealand, a sharp little pull of 1 in 8.33 on Parnell Rise. The second steepest was in Dunedin at Opoho; 1 in 8.81.

The abrupt slopes of the Dunedin hills encouraged that city to be the second in the world to have a cable tramway. To visitors to the city, George Duncan's little trams, gallantly sailing up the slope of Rattray Street, crammed with humanity, were the eighth wonder of the world. For the brave, there was the heart-stopping plunge from the end of the Mornington line down the

Purwodadi station. *(Gedenkboek)*

Wellington's pride, a Fiducia car, is new in 1937. *(Gordon Burt Collection, Alexander Turnbull Library)*

Thoroughly English, a Wellington double-deck car. *(Alexander Turnbull Library)*

The heavy draughthorse helps the tram horses take the strain of this car on a hill in Auckland *(S.C. Smith Collection, Alexander Turnbull Library)*

Queen Street, Auckland. *(Freelance Collection, Alexander Turnbull Library)*

short Maryhill branch, on the steepest cable tramway in the world, — a gradient of 1 in 3.5 compared with the present steepest of 1 in 4.8 on Hyde Street, San Francisco. Although Dunedin prides itself on its Scottish connections, and cable trams were adopted with more enthusiasm in Scotland than in England, they remained something of an oddity, especially as the Mornington cable cars ran for many years on the right-hand side of the road, to the confusion of all other traffic. As late as 1906, contemporaneously with the final expansion of the Edinburgh cable system, antipodean Dunedin was building its last new cable line, and in 1919 work was set in hand for a further extension. If it had been built, this anachronistic adventure would have been the last new line of this type to be built in the world.[3] Similarly to Melbourne, Dunedin built new cable cars until 1924.

Dunedin was the first New Zealand city to see electric trams, in 1900, but soon they had spread to other cities, both metropolitan and provincial. Auckland, Wellington and Christchurch all tried British-style double deckers, but these were never in a majority in any New Zealand tram fleet, despite the English connections of the operators. Some of the larger Wellington cars of the type were known, appropriately, as 'Big Bens'. Auckland actually imported some second-hand tramcars from London, though these were single-deckers. Each system had its own peculiarities. Wellington had its tramway tunnels to pass through the hills, while Auckland could boast two 'grand union' junctions, at the corners where Queen Street met Customs and Wellesley Streets, as well as a 12 kilometre trans-island tramway that linked the east coast at Waitemata Harbour with the west coast at Manukau Harbour. The key to the Auckland system was its principal shopping thoroughfare of Queen Street, which led down to a ferry building with a tower, like a miniature of San Francisco's, where the evening commuters could pour off the lines of trams and onto the *Toroa* or the *Makora* or one of the other ferries for the crossing to the north shore.

There was in Auckland a company that owned both a ferry service and a steam tramway, for land development purposes. Auckland also had a free tram

Roslyn electric tram, 1900. This was New Zealand's first electric line. *(Alexander Turnbull Library)*

shuttle service, later converted to a trolley bus, to service the big Farmers department store whose location was not entirely optimum.

New Zealand was even ahead of Australia in the building of that most characteristic of Australian tram types, the bogie drop-centre. The first of these were designed by Scott Symington, engineer of the Christchurch Tramway Board, to overcome the faults of the previous American-styled trams. Built by the local firm of Boon & Co., the first emerged onto the street in 1906. Dunedin also had some drop-centre trams, but these were imported from Sydney. The more usual New Zealand tram was an end-loading saloon. Many in Auckland had a distinct family resemblance to those in San Francisco.

Among the provincial cities, Wanganui, Invercargill, Napier and New Plymouth all received electric trams, but the most unusual system was in Gisborne. In 1913 this small town adopted, instead of the usual technology, battery-powered trams. As might have been expected from experience elsewhere, the service was not a success, and the trams probably only survived as long as they did because the streets in which they worked were entirely flat.

Like Perth, prams were carried on hooks on the ends of trams in Christchurch and Dunedin. The Birney car was seen in New Zealand a few years before its appearance in Australia. There were three of the type in New Plymouth and six in Invercargill.

The Napier tramways met a violent end on 3 February 1931. On that quiet summer morning the city was shaken by an earthquake so strong that in places the sea became the dry land. Buildings crashed into the street and much of what was left standing was devoured by fire. Motorman Jim Minto, in the centre of a concrete maelstrom, said later that 'the tram was shaken like a fox terrier playing a rat'.[4] Still mourning its hundreds of dead, Napier was to rise again, but the trams had gone forever.

Like England, New Zealand turned away from its trams and towards trolley buses. Christchurch had them in 1931, but Wellington, Auckland, Dunedin and New Plymouth all installed new systems after the war. In Dunedin it was William Goodman, the begetter of the electric tramways, who recommended a wholesale conversion of the system to trolley buses. The trams faded and died, but not without regrets. Both Auckland and Wellington had built new streamlined trams, the last of which had entered service somewhat belatedly in 1952. Some of them now survive in the loving and enthusiastic care of several tramway museums.

The saddest thing was the demise, in 1957, of the Dunedin cable cars, which had even survived the passing of the electric trams. To the tourist visiting the cold and windy streets of Dunedin today, the cable cars would have been an attraction of no mean proportions. Only a few years after they had closed in Dunedin, the citizens of San Francisco gathered to watch the unveiling of a plaque to record that their

Roslyn cable car, loaded with humanity. *(postcard)*

Christchurch steam tram off for a picnic excursion. *(Alexander Turnbull Library)*

Christchurch street scene. *(postcard)*

cable cars were registered as a Historic Landmark by the National Parks Service of the United States Department of the Interior, as possessing 'exceptional value in commemorating and illuminating the history of the United States'.[5] A little more vision at the right time could have prevented the loss to Dunedin of one of its great assets.

To the north of Australia lies Indonesia, once the brightest jewel in the Dutch colonial crown. Here the Dutch railway engineers were able to demonstrate their ability to surmount difficulties not present in their native land, and here also the principal cities had tramways. In Jakarta the first horse trams were opened in 1869, from the Amsterdam Gate at Batavia to Meester Cornelis — now called Pasar Ikan and Jatinegara. The tropical climate took a very heavy toll of the horses, which were replaced by steam in 1882. Steam tramways opened in Semarang and Surabaya soon afterwards. It would not have been unusual to find the steam tram straying far out into the countryside, the little motor with its line of cars puffing between paddy fields and through jungles, or leaping deep rivers on heroic bridges. The last Surabaya steam tram did not clank finally into history until 1978. The steam trams were even useful in keeping the urban thoroughfares clear of market stalls so that other traffic could get through. After electric trams came to Jakarta in 1899 the steam tram company held onto the most lucrative route, which was not converted to electric operation until 1933. Part of a poem by Melis Stoke illustrates the nostalgia of the old Indies hands for the steam trams.

> Then wait I for the coming of
> a close companion to this scene:
> the steamtram, puffing, with a whistle
> on corners, with its bell resounding
> and even in the distance heard . . .[6]

Some visitors were disturbed by the trams' speed and the way their tracks slewed from one side of the road to the other: 'And when these "trams" get up steam, and gallop off at headlong speed, with whistle screaming and bell clanging, round the wide curve at the head of the Molenvliet canal, it is calculated to strike terror into the heart of the bravest'.[7] Alas, Batavia has changed, and 'de oude stoomtram is niet meer'.[8]

Apart from its odd track gauge of 1188 millimetres, Jakarta had a number of other features that would seem strange in Australia or New Zealand. Special open trailers were provided for people bringing their produce to market. Also, although many lines were laid at the sides of the roads, the trams ran on the right on double track, whereas all other traffic kept to the left. With the provision of an electric tram system in Surabaya the Dutch could be proud of their colonies, with their European-style trams running on broad streets between European-style buildings, down to the port where the warships and freighters lay at anchor under their white awnings. Dutch culture was a signpost of civilisation in a developing world.

The Japanese occupation of Indonesia and the subsequent sweeping away of the Dutch administration left the trams intact, but subject to circumstances that would ensure that they would be run until they fell apart, to be replaced by the ubiquitous private 'bemo'. Even the electric railways of Jakarta, once the source of so much Dutch pride, only just survived. It was said that, in their last days, the passengers on the Jakarta trams would come to envy sardines in their cans and that mothers would, on alighting, shake from the pleats of their clothing children squashed flat by the crush.

Further north, in the Malaysian area, lay the British Straits Settlements colonies of Singapore and Penang, both of which had trams, first steam and then electric. In the 1920s they suffered very much from private jitney competition, which led to the early closure of

Hong Kong tram, posed, 1929. *(Tramway and Railway World)*

the Singapore lines and their replacement by what was, for its day, a very large trolley-bus system. In George Town, the port city of the island of Penang, the same progression of events occurred, only a little later. Then, in the 1960s, as the trolley-bus began to lose favour in the British world, so they passed away here also, though in George Town more than 20 years later their routes could still in part be marked by the derelict steel poles that once carried the overhead wires.

In the American colonies of the Philippines there were tramways in Manila and on the fortress island of Corregidor, both destroyed by the fighting in the Second World War. Trams in Manila ran on the left. In the former French colonies, Saigon's trams ceased to be relevant after the war, but those at Hanoi remained until 1990 when they plunged very rapidly into terminal decrepitude. Bangkok, the capital of Thailand, which had the first electric trams in Asia in 1893, saw them succumb to its phenomenal traffic congestion in 1968. Some modernisation was attempted in the 1950s, but the track layout was difficult for a modern city. The list could be almost indefinitely extended with trams present and trams past, but it is appropriate to finish with the last colony, Hong Kong.

When they started in 1905, the Hong Kong trams were just like those of Singapore and George Town, with little crossbench cars running down a 14 kilometre strip between the harbour and the hills. In Wellington, a group of crossbench cars were known as 'Hong Kong' cars because of their resemblance. Unlike those of the other Asian cities, the trams soon became enclosed, and sprouted upper decks, like a little bit of transplanted England. Badly mauled by the war, they nevertheless survived and, in an increasingly crowded city, their services were more and more required. In relative terms, they carry more than twice the passenger loads of Melbourne trams. Today, when almost all the double-deck trams in Britain have vanished, there are still 162 in Hong Kong, covered in brightly-coloured inscrutable Chinese advertising. Until recent years, first class passengers sat on the top deck and second class on the bottom deck. When a typhoon approaches the island, all the trams have to be taken off the road for fear of being blown over. There is nothing much ultra-modern about the Hong Kong trams, though the whole fleet was replaced at the end of the 1980s. Their simplicity, solidity and amenity come first. It was something of a coup for Melbourne, and a justification of its own modernisation policies, to win the contract to build a whole new light railway in Hong Kong's expanding satellite city of Tuen Mun. The first lines, opened in 1988, use 70 new trams, designed in Australia and built in Melbourne and Brisbane. Patronage has risen fast.

14

The People's Carriage

When in 1926 the Melbourne tramways first began to change their colour from chocolate and cream to green and cream, they set a trend that swept through much of the rest of Australia. During the next ten years, trams became green in Sydney, Hobart, Ballarat, Bendigo, Geelong, Perth and Kalgoorlie. The colour in Melbourne, so familiar and predictable, was known simply as Tramway Green on the colour charts. Each city had its own particular shade: light green in Sydney, larch green in Hobart, Bristol green in the Victorian provincial cities — green was the colour. Brisbane and Adelaide were the two big systems not to conform. Brisbane abandoned its browns for silver in 1930 while Adelaide retained its Tuscan red until 1952, when it too opted for silver. In New Zealand, reds were favoured in the majority of cities, but in Australia only Fremantle and Launceston flaunted their defiant red in the face of metropolitan taste for as long as trams lasted. Newcastle, unloved as usual, retained Sydney's previous drab olive and fawn until the end.

In St Peterburg, where there flourishes the modern world's largest tramway system, the trams are painted in a number of different colours so that, as the Russians say, they should be complementary to the beauty of the city itself. In fact, the colour of trams everywhere is of great interest to the people who use them. It is part of their feeling of pride in the place where they live.

When Melbourne obtained the first of its new trams in 1973, it introduced a totally new colour scheme, with a colour officially described as 'Marigold'. This was intended to make them both distinctive and more vividly perceived by the motorists. As people discovered that the Z-class trams were slow to load and stuffy in the summer (though no-one complained about the winter), they were disparagingly referred to as 'clockwork orange' trams after Stanley Kubrick's 1971 film of the same name. The MMTB discovered that their marigold reacted badly to the usual pollution of the city air and that it became difficult to match new paint with old. From 1979, therefore, a lighter colour was introduced, officially called 'Deep Yellow'.

There have always been trams decorated for various occasions and for patriotic purposes. Ballarat and Bendigo were noted for each having a tram decorated at Christmas as a 'Santa Special'. In Bendigo, Santa Claus would arrive at Myers at the start of the Christmas season in his gorgeously decorated tram, while at Ballarat a tram made up to look like a paddle steamer would pitch gently as it ran under the trees beside the lake. Melbourne did things in style with a tram that was decorated like fairyland with lights all round its roof. This tram was hired for advertising campaigns, first appearing in 1958, and then on a permanent basis from 1970. Glowing like a beacon in the streets, it was not without one small problem. Every driver is told in the school in which he learns to drive a tram that, when a tram comes to a power-operated set of facing points, he should switch off the power to go straight ahead and leave the power on to go around the corner. As a simple aide-memoire he has only to remember his wife, who drives him round the bend, and in the same way, he should coast to go straight ahead but drive the tram round. The illuminated tram drew so much power for its lights that the simple automatic equipment would never recognise it as wishing to go straight ahead, and it would change every set of points it came to. The driver would then have to be get out and change them back again with his points iron.

The homely trams are the scene of much social interchange, from the case of Mr J. Trethowan, of the SEC, who met his wife on the Mount Pleasant tram, to Rebecca Batties, noting in *The Age* in 1981 how many elderly ladies in minks, clutching their pensioner concessions, caught the East Malvern tram. One nice vignette I saw on the East Preston tram early in 1982. The ticket inspectors are usually hard-faced men who get that way from constantly having people trying to put one over them, but on this occasion it was quite an attractive woman. One man who she approached had a pocket full of tickets from previous trips and had difficulty in finding the right one. When he finally had it he asked her, 'What do I win with this?' 'A smile,' she replied. There are other events that one recalls with a smile; among them garrulous men who want to engage all the other passengers in discussion

Elizabeth Street. *(C. Jones)*

Silent Sunday morning in Melbourne by the Princess Theatre. *(C. Jones)*

1041 in its first colour scheme. *(C. Jones)*

A-class tram. *(C. Jones)*

Tram in William Street. *(C. Jones)*

Tram at Arts Centre. *(C. Jones)*

Bill Johnson retires at the age of 65 in May 1983, after 42 years on the trams. *(Herald and Weekly Times)*

about the current fortunes of the local football team, or the occasion when the tram was coming down Clarendon Street driven by a veritable Fangio of the rails. The connie was unprepared for a turn at speed at Albert Park, and although I said 'Mind the curve', she landed rather abruptly in my lap.

The story is told about the old days in Sydney, when a larrikin factory girl coming home on the tram from Botany or Mascot would pick up a used ticket and tuck it into the leg elastic of her bloomers, so that the serial number was hidden. The inspector, as he swung along the outside of the crossbench car calling 'Show tickets, please', would be shown a shapely leg but would never put his hand as far as the bloomer elastic.

Another story concerns the tram from Glenelg that had to stop because there were two dogs on the line 'producing their offspring'. Nothing would shift them until the conductor went to an adjacent house to obtain a bucket of water.[1]

Every so often there will be a drunk aboard who will refuse to pay his fare. The other passengers will then be treated to a small play in several acts, during which the conductor's persuasion will be met by truculence, as will be the arrival of the driver in support. Next the tram may be driven as far as the place where an inspector may be found and, if his presence is also of no use, he must go and phone for the police to take the offender into custody. The passengers pay for this little play by being somewhat late in arriving at wherever they were going. One resourceful conductor met a drunk on the Wattle Park tram in 1972 in similar circumstances. This one had a carton of beer with him, and when the drunk refused either to pay his fare or get off the tram the conductor grabbed his carton and put it down in the gutter. A cry of 'come and get it' quickly had the drunk off the tram and the situation resolved.

An accumulation of such incidents can make a piece of theatre, and so was born *Storming Mont Albert by Tram*, a show which has never been entirely out of production for a number of years.

Barry Dickins, contemplating lunch on the restaurant tram, recalled that 'People always eat on trams. I have seen Greek families hop into pots of hot stew, unselfconsciously gnawing a leg of goat on the tram to East Coburg or Ascot Vale. You've got to keep warm somehow on those windy and sometimes doorless relics. Get some goat into you!'[2]

Even today, when much of society seems to be

Boarding tram, Bourke Street Mall. *(C. Jones)*

becoming so impersonal, the little world of the trams retains something of an old-fashioned warmth. The platform staff become well known and one can give a word of sympathy to the conductor in his overcoat, having had to take the first car out of the depot at 5 a.m. on a frosty morning, or have a chat on the way into town in the evening, when things are a bit quiet. The motorist, isolated in the peak-hour crowd of his peers, must miss the leisurely scanning of the morning paper and the daily contact with friends, and the familiar strangers, on the trams.

A certain rush of emotion about the trams was evidenced at Bendigo after the closure of the system in 1972. One of the Birney cars had been promised to the tramway museum in the state in which it had first run, South Australia, but when the museum society members arrived to collect it, they found the local group had welded a pipe across the tracks, stolen their lifting jacks and changed the locks on the depot. In a day of drama, the mayor of Bendigo announced that he would call for help on the local radio station to prevent any attempt being made to move the tram. Subsequent events resulted in the establishment of Bendigo's tourist tramway, but the ill-feeling generated between Bendigo and the other museum groups was not dissipated until 1976, when a different Birney was rescued from a farm and brought back to running order for donation to the Adelaide group.

The old joke used to have it that the Tramways Board runs its business on good lines. A new Victorian government decided that something new was required, and on 30 June 1983 the Melbourne and Metropolitan Tramways Board ceased to exist and was replaced by the more modern-sounding Metropolitan Transit Authority, a body which would also administer the suburban railway system. The tramway employees joked anxiously about whether they had taken over the railways or had been taken over by them. In fact it was a move that was to leave the tramways exposed to future political winds. At the outset, though, the plans showed a victory for the trams in the urban area. The St Kilda and Port Melbourne railway lines, so nearly closed under the previous administration, were converted to tramways, and to run on these lines the first articulated trams in Australia were built.

The old trams were beginning to vanish from the streets in favour of the new. The last official service by a W2-class vehicle was in December 1987. The first tram in Australia to reach 60 years in service was No.223, in 1984. The new trams were not before time.

But things were far from well with the tramways, and the search for cost savings extended in many directions. First there was the matter of staff and ticketing. During 1989 there were firm moves to start the phasing-out of conductors, and the operation of one-man trams. Hand in hand with this went a new type of 'scratch' ticket, bought from agencies and validated by the passenger. It must have seemed like a good idea at the time. The tramway union reacted in no uncertain terms, and there was a series of stoppages and disruptions as the details of the new scheme became clear. Lou Di Gregorio, secretary of

This Ron Tandberg cartoon says it all, 2 October 1974. *(The Age)*

the union, aimed to wreck the new ticket system, and the union members were prepared for a long campaign. It was to be one of the most bitter ever. The new tickets were used in tandem with the old in December, but as from 1 January 1990 the whole new system was to be in place. Platform staff declared a free travel day on that day, but a complete breakdown between management and union saw over 200 trams driven out of their depots around midnight and parked in the central city streets. Management subsequently turned off the power, and the trams were left there for five weeks. City businesses reported drops in sales of up to 25 per cent, with losses totalling $10 million.

There was a fiery meeting at Brunswick Town Hall on 2 February, attended by 1200 union members. Most voted for a return to work, but services were not back to 80 per cent of timetable for another week. Who won? It is very doubtful if the answer to that question would be 'the people.'

There was also a disturbing trend for the mindless graffiti writers, who had been for so long the bane of the railways, to extend their efforts to the trams.

There were other battles that year too, such as the successful campaign to prevent the conversion of the much under-patronised Upfield railway to light rail, with the introduction of modern low-floor trams. It seemed as though the whole political consensus on which the tramway system rested had been broken. To many, it seemed that the union was now in charge. The change which brought in the Kennett Government in 1992 saw the battle joined again for the abolition of conductors.[3] It was to a great extent the solid good sense of the negotiations between the transport minister, Alan Brown, and the union, that resolved the issue in a satisfactory manner.

One man who spoke out was Patrick O'Connor, of the Public Transport Users Association. He it was who 'hijacked' the tram to St Kilda when it was being short-shunted in 1985. 'A contract had been entered into to take us to St Kilda Beach,' Mr O'Connor said. 'I ordered the driver to take us to our destination. He

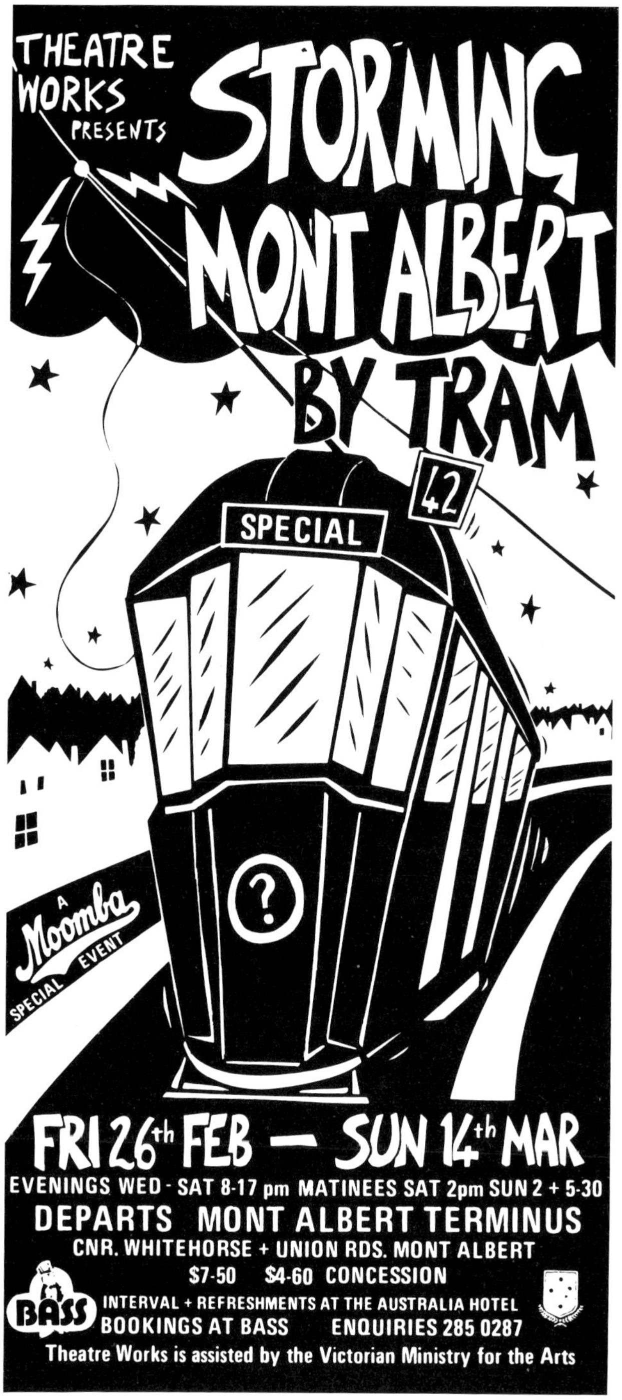

Storming Mont Albert by Tram poster, 1982. *(C. Jones collection)*

shouted at me and I shouted at him.'[4] His voice was heard on many occasions, and in a modern world where management has been substantially corporatised, he is much more authentically the voice of the people.

For the trams are still 'the people's carriage', just as they were to George Train, back in 1861, and there is no doubt that the Melbourne trams, whether or not they are sold to overseas banks and leased back by the operator, really belong to the people of Melbourne. Green and gold in the streets, classified (in part) by the National Trust, they are very much a part of Melbourne's character, Melbourne's pride.

Appendix 1
Australasian Tramways

City	*State*	*In operation*	*Max. length*	*Max. trams*	*Gauge*
Electric tramways					
Melbourne	Vic.	1906 to date	238.0 km	839	1435 mm& 1600 mm
Adelaide	S.A.	1909 to date[a]	133.3 km	311	1435 mm
Brisbane	Qld	1897–1969	108.4 km	428	1435 mm
Sydney	N.S.W.	1893–1961	264.0 km	1499	1435 mm
Hobart	Tas.	1893–1960	26.9 km	79	1067 mm
Wellington	N.Z.	1904–64	52.8 km	225	1219 mm
Jakarta	Java	1899–1962	30.6 km	74	1188 mm
Auckland	N.Z.	1902–56	72.0 km	231	1435 mm
Perth	W.A.	1899–1958	92.2 km	159	1067 mm
Bendigo	Vic.	1903–72[b]	13.9 km	25	1435 mm
Geelong	Vic.	1912–56	19.0 km	31	1435 mm
Manila	Luzon	1905–45	54.5 km	133	1435 mm
Surabaya	Java	1923–68	18.0 km	37	1067 mm
Newcastle	N.S.W.	1923–50	38.2 km	98	1435 mm
Launceston	Tas.	1911–52	19.7 km	29	1067 mm
Ballarat	Vic.	1905–71[b]	22.3 km	27	1435 mm
Wanganui	N.Z.	1908–50	23.0 km	17	1435 mm
Christchurch	N.Z.	1905–54	86.1 km	92	1435 mm
Corregidor	Luzon	1910–42	7.2 km	11	914 mm
Kalgoorlie	W.A.	1902–52	23.9 km	25	1067 mm
Dunedin	N.Z.	1900–56	27.0 km	62	1422 mm& 1067 mm
George Town	Penang	1906–36	16.0 km	21	1067 mm
New Plymouth	N.Z.	1916–54	10.8 km	10	1435 mm
Napier	N.Z.	1913–31	7.4 km	9	1067 mm
Singapore	Singa.	1905–29	25.5 km	60	1067 mm
Invercargill	N.Z.	1912–52	12.0 km	16	1435 mm
Leonora	W.A.	1908–16[c]	4.0 km	1	1067 mm
Horse tramways					
Victor Harbor	S.A.	1894–1955	3.1 km	2	1600 mm
		1986 to date	1.8 km	4	1600 mm
Broome	W.A.	1902–10[e]	5.2 km	2	1067 mm
Gawler	S.A.	1879–1931	2.0 km	2	1600 mm
Adelaide	S.A.	1878–1917	89.9 km	170	1435 mm& 1600 mm
Christchurch	N.Z.	1882–1914[f]	32.8 km	54	1435 mm
Moonta	S.A.	1896–1931	8.3 km	9	1600 mm

Appendix 1 (contd)

City	State	In operation	Max. length	Max. trams	Gauge
Cable tramways					
Melbourne	Vic.	1885–1940	74.0 km	592	1435 mm
Dunedin	N.Z.	1881–1957	8.0 km	20	1067 mm
Sydney	N.S.W.	1886–1905	7.3 km	41	1435 mm
Steam tramways					
Broome	W.A.	1910–42[g]	5.2 km	4	1067 mm
Auckland	N.Z.	1910–27	11.4 km	7	1435 mm
Newcastle	N.S.W.	1887–1932	55.5 km	52	1435 mm
Batavia	Java	1883–1934	6.6 km	38	1188 mm
Rockhampton[d]	Qld	1909–39	19.1 km	11	1067 mm
Surabaya	Java	1889–1978	20.1 km	24	1067 mm
Broken Hill	N.S.W.	1902–26	16.2 km	13	1435 mm
Parramatta	N.S.W.	1883–1943	15.7 km	9	1435 mm
Sydney	N.S.W.	1879–1937	77.0 km	110	1435 mm
Maitland	N.S.W.	1893–1926	12.3 km	7	1435 mm
Semarang	Java	1882–1940	11.7 km	16	1067 mm
Christchurch	N.Z.	1880–1914	20.9 km	8	1435 mm
Zeehan	Tas.	1893–1919	3.6 km	2	610 mm
Leonora	W.A.	1903–08	4.0 km	1	1067 mm
Bendigo	Vic.	1892–1903	6.2 km	8	1435 mm
Battery tramways					
Gisborne	N.Z.	1913–29	5.5 km	4	1219 mm

[a] 90% of system closed by 1958.
[b] Tourist operations run on part of original system.
[c] Continued to 1921 with one petrol tram.
[d] Includes 'railway trams'.
[e] 610-mm gauge to 1907.
[f] Some sections run with steam on occasion.
[g] Reopened 1946–54 with one petrol tram.

Note that the above list includes only those tramways that invested in new track or rolling stock after 1896, and listing is in that order. Separate systems in the one city are shown combined, and permanently coupled tramcars are counted as one unit. For steam and cable tramways, the numbers refer to motors and dummies only. Kilometres include regular routes as well as other trackage.

Appendix 2
Australasian Tramways from 1938: Major New Construction

Melbourne

Route extensions

Bulleen Road to North Balwyn	1.3 km	11 December 1938
Maribyrnong River to West Maribyrnong	2.2 km	22 December 1940
Raleigh's Road to Ordnance Factory	0.7 km	6 July 1941
Ascot Vale to Moonee Ponds	1.3 km	24 May 1942
Essendon North to Essendon Aerodrome	2.4 km	16 May 1942
William Street to Hanna Street	1.8 km	3 February 1946
LaTrobe Street line	2.5 km	15 January 1951
Ordnance Factory to Cordite Factory	1.4 km	2 May 1954
Bourke Street to Northcote	9.9 km	26 June 1955[a]
Exhibition to East Brunswick	4.3 km	8 April 1956[b]
Queens Way deviation	0.8 km	21 October 1968
Burwood to East Burwood	3.4 km	20 July 1978
East Preston to Reservoir	1.2 km	18 May 1983
Reservoir to LaTrobe University	2.1 km	10 January 1985
LaTrobe University to Bundoora	2.9 km	26 April 1987
Whiteman Street to St Kilda	4.4 km	22 November 1987[c]
Port Junction to Port Melbourne	2.5 km	20 December 1987[c]
Airport West extension	1.2 km	22 December 1992
East Burwood extension	1.7 km	June 1993
Bundoora to Mill Park	1.0 km	

[a] Reinstatement of former cable-tram route.
[b] Reinstatement and extension of former cable-tram route.
[c] Replacement of heavy rail by light rail.

New tramcars

W5 class	Nos 797–798, 802–807 & 821–839	1938–39
W6 type	Nos 840–979 & 981–1000	1939–55
VR class	Nos 52–54	1942 (Elwood line)
PCC type	No 980	1950
W7 class	Nos 1001–1040	1955–56
Z type	Nos 1–115	1975–79
Z3 class	Nos 116–230	1979–84
A type	Nos 231–300	1984–87
B class	Nos 2001–2002	1985–86
B2 class	Nos 2003–2132	1988–93

New depots

East Preston	1955
North Fitzroy	1956

Adelaide

Route extensions

Fullarton to Springfield		1.4 km	8 July 1938
Hilton to Richmond		1.9 km	29 June 1939
Kilkenny to Cheltenham		2.3 km	12 April 1942
Marryatville to Erindale		1.6 km	14 January 1944
Franklin Street loop		0.8 km	9 February 1952

New tramcar

H1 class	No 381		1953

New depot

Goodwood	1986		

Brisbane

Route extensions

Lutwyche to Stafford		2.3 km	27 January 1940
Moorooka to Salisbury		2.2 km	22 September 1941
Lutwyche Cemetery to Chermside		1.5 km	29 March 1947
Camp Hill to Belmont		1.5 km	31 July 1948
Newmarket to Enoggera		2.1 km	15 August 1949
Holland Park to Nursery Road		1.5 km	13 November 1950
Nursery Road to Mount Gravatt		1.1 km	14 March 1951
O'Keefe Street link		0.7 km	9 March 1961

New tramcars

200 type	Nos 369–386		1938
400 type	Nos 400–473		1938–47
400 type	Nos 474–554		1947–64

Sydney

New tramcars

R1 class	Nos 1988–2087		1950–53

Wellington

Route extension

Bowen Street link		0.8 km	2 August 1940

New tramcars

Fiducia class	Nos 235–260		1938–53

Hobart

New tramcars

100 type	Nos 114–118 & 121–142		1938–52

Auckland

Route extension

Epsom to Greenlane		0.6 km	29 April 1939

New tramcars

Streamliner	Nos 247–256		1938–43

Bendigo

Route extension

Lake Weeroona to North Bendigo		1.2 km	23 November 1942

Perth

Route extension

Victoria Park to Welshpool	1.4 km	21 September 1942

New tramcar

A type	No 36	1939 (Fremantle)

Note that the above listings include only completely new tramcars and track extensions of over 0.5 km.

Painted tram No. 607 by Craig Gough. 'I visualised the tram as an exciting and joyous object only seen briefly as it trundled past.' *(C. Jones)*

At the tram parade, 1991. *(C. Jones)*

Light Rail Vehicle in Middle Park. *(C. Jones)*

Adelaide trams in silver paint, coupled for the evening rush, 1973. *(C. Jones)*

Christmas tram. *(C. Jones)*

Light Rail Vehicle in Bourke Street Mall. *(C. Jones)*

Painting the tram, 1991. *(C. Jones)*

The great tram strike of 1990, with trams lining all the city streets. *(C. Jones)*

Sam the Tram. *(C. Jones)*

Imagery of peace and happiness on this tram painted by the renowned cartoonist, Michael Leunig. *(C. Jones)*

3KZ publicity sticker. *(Courtesy KZFM Radio Pty Ltd)*

Notes

Chapter 1: The American Invention

1. *Sydney Morning Herald* 24 December 1861.
2. Petition dated 10 June 1862 in *New South Wales Parliamentary Papers.*
3. *New South Wales Parliamentary Papers*, 1873-74, *Sydney and Suburban Streets Tramway Bill.*

Chapter 2: Iron Rails in Adelaide

1. Permanent London tramways commenced in 1870.
2. Tramways have ever since been responsible for the upkeep of a substantial section of the centre of the road — about 6 metres width for a double track line. It came to be seen in later years as one more crippling imposition.
3. The usual maximum on modern electric lines is 3.7 metres.
4. *South Australian Parliamentary Papers*, 1876, No.49, *Adelaide & Suburban Tramways Bill.*
5. L. Kingsborough, *The Horse Tramways of Adelaide*, 1967, Appendix 1.
6. Quoted in Thistle Anderson, *Arcadian Adelaide*, 1905, p. 20.

Chapter 3: Steam in the Streets

1. *New South Wales Parliamentary Papers*, 1877-78, *Sydney Tramway and Omnibus Company (Limited) Bill.*
2. *Ibid.*
3. *New South Wales Parliamentary Papers*, 1879-80, *Tramways Extension Bill.*
4. *Ibid., Sydney City and Suburban Tramway and Omnibus Company's Bill.*
5. *Ibid.*
6. G. V. Portus, *Happy Highways*, 1953, p. 6.
7. *New South Wales Debates*, 13 September 1882, p. 383.
8. *Newcastle Morning Herald*, 6 July 1887.
9. J. Dixon, *History of Merewether*, 1935, p. 49.
10. K. McCarthy, 'Working on the Trams in the 1880s', *Trolley Wire*, February 1981.
11. *An Anthology of Australian Verse*, chosen by George Mackaness, 1952, p. 292.

Chapter 4: Cable Car

1. *The Age*, 4 August 1882.
2. *Victorian Parliamentary Papers*, 1882-83, *The Melbourne Tramway and Omnibus Company's Bill.*
3. *The Argus*, 28 October 1885.
4. The date is significant in Australian history for other events: 1881 — the hanging of Ned Kelly; 1918 — the Armistice in the Great War; 1975 — the dismissal of the Whitlam Government.
5. Graham McInnes, *The Road to Gundagai*, 1967, p. 69.
6. Frank Hardy, *Power Without Glory*, 1968, p. 435.
7. Quoted in *Tall Stories*, from a contribution by a member of the 3DB Tall Story Club, no date.
8. Not as bad, however, as the situation in the famous San Francisco poem of Gelett Burgess: Two-and-twenty 'let-go's' every double trip — It takes a bit of doing, on the Hyde Street Grip.

Chapter 5: An Electric Spark

1. *The Age* 15 October 1889.
2. 'Hold the Fort!' by P.P. Bliss was Hymn No.1 in *Sacred Songs and Solos*, compiled by Ira D. Sankey.
3. *Tasmanian Parliamentary Papers* 1884, No.150.
4. *Pugh's Almanac*, 1893.
5. *Sydney Morning Herald*, 9 December 1899.
6. K. McCarthy, 'The Introduction of the O-Class Tramcars — 1908', *Trolley Wire*, December 1978.

Chapter 6: The Staple of Urban Life

1. Noted on a postcard, in *The Australian Tram*, Sydney 1969.
2. G. Casey and T. Mayman, *The Mile that Midas Touched*, 1964, p. 199.
3. *The Argus*, 18 January 1911.
4. T. Wood, *Cobbers*, 1931, p. 35.
5. *Mercury*, 9 July 1892.

Chapter 7: The Management and the Union

1. *Victorian Parliamentary Papers*, 1882-83, *The Melbourne Tramway and Omnibus Company's Bill.*
2. *The Argus*, 17 August, 1910
3. *Victorian Parliamentary Papers*, 1898, *Tramway Employés Grievances.*
4. *The Argus*, 16 August, 1910.
5. *The Argus*, 19 August, 1910.
6. *The Argus*, 3 December 1910.
7. Restated in a speech for the hundredth anniversary of the cable tramways, Richmond Town Hall, 11 November 1985.

Chapter 8: Something New

1. *The Argus*, 7 May 1906.
2. *The Argus*, 15 March 1937.
3. 'Official Bulletin No.9', quoted in 'Joseph Stillman Badger', *Trolley Wire*, December 1977.
4. Reprinted in R. Willson, D. Keenan and R. Henderson, *The Green Lines*, 1966, and reproduced here with permission.
5. *Daily Telegraph*, 9 December 1926.
6. Data is representative only, as growth in population and tramway penetration, as well as economic events, affected figures as the decade progressed.

Chapter 9: Something Old

1. Recalled by Commander Ron Pedder, RAN, in *The Three-Headed Dog*, June 1987.
2. The first Birney car ran in Seattle in 1916.
3. In Bendigo in the mid-1960s, relative patronage was at only half the level of Brisbane, and it declined rapidly thereafter.
4. T. Wood, *Cobbers*, 1931, p.158.
5. *The Age*, 28 October 1983.

Chapter 10: Falling Leaves

1. Quoted in 'Exit — Perth's Trolley Buses', *Trolley Wire*, February 1970.
2. *The Mercury*, 27 November 1934.
3. It was sponsored by the department store, Allan and Stark, now Myer. Myer also opened a big suburban development about the same time at Chadstone, in Melbourne.
4. R. Wheaton, *Rails to the Bay*, 1971, p. 61.
5. The last trams ran in Paris in 1938, London in 1952 and New York in 1955. The last route extensions in both London and Sydney were in 1932, but the decision to scrap was taken in London in 1931.

Chapter 11: Farewell Brisbane Ladies

1. *Courier Mail*, 6 November 1952.
2. *Ibid.*
3. The PCC was at this time the basis for substantial new construction in Europe.
4. Definitely no relation of the author!
5. *Walkabout*, March 1971.

Chapter 12: Trams are Here to Stay

1. T. Wood, *Cobbers*, 1931, p. 157.
2. *The Argus*, 29 June 1955.
3. In the event the underground railway was cripplingly expensive, and finished hugely behind schedule.
4. *Herald*, 24 October 1978.
5. The tram is now owned by the Museum of Victoria, and has been restored to Pugh's original paintwork.
6. Robert Risson retired in 1970, but served as executive director of the Metropolitan Transportation Committee until 1975. He died in 1992.
7. In world terms, it ranks about eleventh.

Chapter 13: Trams International

1. The trams sold to Seattle were Melbourne's oldest, yet they were the most modern tramcars ever seen in that city.
2. From *The Dominion*, quoted in *Tramway Topics*, April 1984.
3. Melbourne built a short-lived deviation in Lonsdale Street in 1924, and the San Francisco system was rebuilt in its entirety in 1983.
4. G. Stewart, *The End of the Penny Section*, 1973, p. 154.
5. Part of the citation, attached to the engine house in 1964.
6. Author's translation from 'Bataviaasche impressie', in H. Duparc, *De Elektrische Stadstrams op Java*, 1972, p. 17.
7. H. W. Ponder, *Java Pageant*, 1934, p. 26.
8. 'Bataviaasche impressie', in Duparc, op cit.

Chapter 14: The People's Carriage

1. H. Gelsen, *Fares Please!*, 1983, pp. 43-44.
2. *Business Review Weekly*, 17-23 September 1983.
3. The unusually long preservation of the conductors' role is indicated by comparison with San Francisco, which voted to end mandatory two-man operation in 1954.
4. *The Age*, 7 December 1985.

Select Bibliography

Historians of tramways have been particularly active in publication, both in enthusiast magazines and in books. This list indicates the tip of this technical and historical iceberg, to which I am much indebted. Material below is arranged geographically.

Australia

Sydney

G. Andrews, *The Ferries of Sydney*, Reed, Sydney, 1975

I. Brady, *Eastern Suburbs Railway*, ARHS, Sydney, 1979

L. Clark, *North of the Harbour*, Newey and Beath, Newcastle, 1976

W. Denham, *Tramway Byways, North Sydney*, SPER, Sydney, 1973

W. Denham, (ed.), *Sydney Tramway Museum*, SPER, Sydney, 1986

S. Dornan and R. Henderson, *The Electric Railways of New South Wales*, AETA, Sydney, 1976

R. Henderson, 'Bondi Via Bel'Vue', *Electric Traction*, January-February 1965

R. Henderson, 'Sydney Harbour Bridge Jubilee', *Electric Traction*, March-April 1982

D. Keenan, *Tramways of Sydney*, Transit, Sydney, 1979

D. Keenan, *The South-Eastern Lines*, Transit, Sydney, 1982

D. Keenan, *The North Sydney Lines*, Transit, Sydney, 1987

D. Keenan, *The Ryde Line*, Transit, Sydney, 1988

D. Keenan, *The Eastern Lines*, Transit, Sydney, 1989

D. Keenan, *The Watson's Bay Line*, Transit, Sydney, 1990

D. Keenan, *City Lines*, Transit, Sydney, 1991

D. Keenan, *The South-Western Lines*, Transit, Sydney, 1992

I. MacCowan, *The Sydney Trolley Bus*, published privately, Melbourne, 1988

I. MacCowan, *The Tramways of New South Wales*, published privately, Melbourne, 1990

L. Manny and B. Irwin, *Past and Present*, Steam & Railway Preservation (Co-op) Soc. Ltd, Sydney, c.1979

K. McCarthy, 'The NSW Trolley Bus Era', *Electric Traction*, August 1962-March 1963

K. McCarthy and N. Chinn, *A Century of New South Wales Tramcars*, SPER, Sydney, Vol 2. 1968

K. McCarthy and N. Chinn, *New South Wales Tramcar Handbook*, SPER, Sydney, part 1. 1975, part 2. 1976

K. McCarthy, 'The Destruction of an Asset', *Trolley Wire*, October 1977 - February 1978

K. McCarthy, 'The Manly Tramways', *Trolley Wire* from October 1979 (series not finished)

K. McCarthy, 'Reaching the North Shore', *Trolley Wire*, April-June 1982

K. McCarthy, 'North Sydney Cable Tramway Centenary', *Trolley Wire*, April-June 1986

J. Richardson, *Destination Circular Quay*, Traction, Canberra, 1967

C. Thomas, *In and Around Sydney with the Steam Tram*, Book 3, Steam Tram & Railway Preservation Society, Sydney, 1961

G. Travers, *The Australian Double Decker*, Historic Commercial Vehicle Assoc, Sydney, 1977

R. Willson, 'The Line that was Suspension Bridge', *Electric Traction*, November-December 1967

R. Willson, 'Experimental Twins', *Electric Traction*, June - July 1971

R. Willson, 'The Sydney Corridor Tramcars', *Electric Traction*, December 1972-August 1973

R. Willson, R. Henderson and D. Keenan, *The Red Lines*, AETA, Sydney 1970

R. Willson, D. Keenan and R. Henderson, *The Enfield Lines*, AETA, Sydney, 1971

R. Wylie, 'The Cable Tramways of Sydney', *ARHS Bulletin*, July - August 1974

Melbourne

G. Breydon, *Feeding and Filling*, TMSV, Melbourne, 1990

J. Cranston, *The Melbourne Cable Trams 1885-1940*, Craftsman, Melbourne, 1988

N. Cross and K. Kings, *Destination City*, AETA, Sydney, 1981

D. Dunstan, *Governing the Metropolis*, MUP, Melbourne, 1984

M. Fiddian, *Clang, Clang, Clang*, Pakenham Gazette, Pakenham, 1993

R. Green, *The First Electric Road*, John Mason, Melbourne, 1989
P. Haseldine, 'By Tram to Kew in '82', *Modern Tramway*, May-August 1982
C. Jones, H. Ballment and P. Nicholson, 'The Lonie Report', *Electric Traction*, December 1980-February 1981
J. Keating, *Mind the Curve*, MUP, Melbourne, 1970
D. Keenan, *Melbourne Tramways in 1974*, Transit, Sydney, 1974
D. Keenan, *Melbourne Tramways*, Transit, Sydney, 1985
K. Kings, '60 Years of the MMTB', *Trolley Wire*, December 1979-April 1980
L. Marshall-Wood, 'The Development of the Melbourne Tramways', *The Modern Tramway*, March-April 1948
L. Marshall-Wood, *The Brighton Electric Line*, Traction, Canberra, 1966
K. McCarthy, 'Melbourne Tramway Centenary', *Trolley Wire*, October-December 1985
J. Moir, *Australia's First Electric Tram*, Traction, Canberra, 1961
J. Prideaux, '50 Years of Preston Workshops', *Electric Traction*, October-November 1975
J. Richardson, *The Essendon Tramways*, Traction, Canberra, 1964
G. Serle, *The Rush to be Rich*, MUP, Melbourne, 1971

Brisbane
H. Clark and D. Keenan, *Brisbane Tramways, the Last Decade*, Transit, Sydney, 1977
J. Cole, *Shaping a City*, William Brooks, Brisbane, 1984
G. Ford, 'Joseph Stillman Badger', *Trolley Wire*, December 1977-April 1978
R. Lawson, *Brisbane in the 1890s*, UQP, Brisbane, 1973
J. Richardson, *Destination Valley*, Traction, Canberra, 1964

Adelaide
C. Andrews, L. Fenner, J. Hoffmann and R. White, *The Tramway Museum, St Kilda, SA*, AETA, Adelaide, 1982
H. Gelsen, *Fares Please!*, Investigator, Adelaide, 1983
L. Kingsborough, *The Horse Tramways of Adelaide and its Suburbs*, Libraries Board of SA, Adelaide, 1967
C. Steele, 'Adelaide Trolley Bus Services', *Electric Traction*, December 1963-February 1964
C. Steele and R. Wheaton, *Adelaide on the Move*, AETA, Sydney, 1978
C. Steele, 'A Brief History of Street Transport in Adelaide', *Electric Traction*, April-November 1979
C. Steele, *The Burnside Lines*, AETA, Sydney, 1981
C. Steele, *From Omnibus to O-Bahn*, AETA, Adelaide, 1986
R. Wheaton, *Rails to the Bay*, AETA, Sydney, 1971
R. Wheaton, *Destination Paradise*, AETA, Sydney, 1975

Western Australia
T. Bell, 'Trams on the Golden Mile', *Tramway Topics*, April-December 1982
J. Richardson, *Destination Subiaco*, Traction, Canberra, 1967
G. Stewart, *Urban Transport and the MTT*, Charles Amery, Perth, c.1981

Tasmania
J. Chesworth, I. Cooper, P. James and J. Stokes, *The Electric Tramways of Hobart*, AETA, Sydney, 1960
I. Cooper, *Trolley Buses of Tasmania*, AETA, Sydney, 1979
L. Rae, *A History of Railways and Tramways on Tasmania's West Coast*, privately published, Hobart, 1983
J. Richardson, *Destination GPO*, Traction, Canberra, 1971

Provincial New South Wales
K. McCarthy, 'Newcastle Tramways', *Trolley Wire* from February 1977 (series not completed)
K. McCarthy, *Steaming down Argent Street*, Sydney Tramway Museum, Sydney, 1983
R. Willson and K. McCarthy, *Maitland Tramway Ventures*, SPER, Sydney, 1965

Provincial Victoria
B. Andrews, *By Birney to Golden Square*, Southern Cross Traction, Adelaide, 1973
K. Kings, *Destination Eaglehawk*, Traction, Canberra, 1965
K. Kings, *The Ballarat Tramways*, ARHS, Melbourne, 1971
K. Kings, *The Bendigo Tramways*, ARHS, Melbourne, 1972
S. Mackinnon, *Bendigo and its Talking Trams*, Bendigo Trust, Bendigo, 1981
B. Prentice, *The Reconstruction of the Victorian Provincial Tramways*, privately published, Haddon, 1976
A. Winzenried, *Tram to Sorrento*, APW, Belgrave, 1984

Provincial Queensland
J. Knowles, 'The Rockhampton City Tramways', *ARHS Bulletin*, June - September 1974
K. McCarthy, 'Rockhampton Tramways', *Trolley Wire*, June 1972-August 1973

J. Nicholson, *Rocky's 'Puffing Billies'*, published privately, Rockhampton, 1988

Provincial South Australia

K. McCarthy, 'Country Horse Tramways in South Australia', *Trolley Wire*, October 1980-November 1987

New Zealand

M. Alexander, *Rails in the Roads*, Christchurch Transport Board & Tramway Historical Society, Christchurch, 1985

R. Alexander, 'Wanganui Tramways', *Tramway Topics*, September/October 1972-January/February 1973

D. Balderston, *The Harbour Ferries of Auckland*, Grantham House, Wellington, 1986

B. Dale, D. Hinman, J. Shanks, I Spicer and D. Jones, *All Fares Please*, Tramway Historical Society, Christchurch, 1967

G. Ditchfield, 'Endless Wire Rope Traction in Dunedin NZ, *Tramway Topics*, May/June 1971-July/August 1974

D. Greenhill, 'Wellington Tramway System', *Tramway Topics*, August 1983-February 1984

T. Headifen, 'Behind the Scenes of the Wellington Electric Tramways', *Tramway Topics*, July/August 1974-March/April 1975

J. Kenneally, *By Toe and Straphold*, John McIndoe, Dunedin, 1979

M. Kerr, 'Christchurch Tram Routes', *Tramway Topics*, Sep/Oct 1971-January/February 1973

B. Maffey, 'Christchurch Tramway Accidents', *Tramway Topics*, July/August 1973-March/April 1975

I. Maffey, 'Christchurch's Victorian Tramways', *Tramway Topics*, April 1984-April 1985

T. McGarvin, *Wellington Tramway Memories*, NZRLS, Wellington, 1978

D. McQueen, 'Gisborne Tramways', *Tramway Topics*, July/August-October 1989

S. Millar, *Trolleybuses in New Zealand*, Millar, Auckland, 1986

C. Steele, 'A Visitor's View of New Zealand in 1965', *Electric Traction*, January-February 1966

G. Stewart, *The End of the Penny Section*, Reed, Wellington, 1973

G. Stewart, *When Trams Were Trumps in New Zealand*, Grantham House, Wellington, 1985

Indonesia

S. Abeyasekere, *Jakarta: A History*, Oxford, Singapore, 1987

H. Duparc, *De Elektrische Stadstrams op Java*, Wyt, Rotterdam, 1972

Gedenkboek der Samarang-Joana Stoomtram-Maatschappij, Gravenhage, 1907

Philippines

Manila Electric Company, official history, Manila, 1976

C. Small, *Rails to Doomsday*, Railroad Monographs, Greenwich CT, 1980

Hong Kong

R. Atkinson and A. Williams, *Hongkong Tramways*, LRTL, Rustington, 1970

M. Barnett, *Tramlines*, South China Morning Post, Hong Kong, 1984

T. Runnacles, 'Tramway Developments in Hong Kong', *Modern Tramway*, August 1988-October 1990

Other and General

R. Buckley, *History of Tramways*, David and Charles, Newton Abbott, 1975

S. Carlson and F. Schneider, *PCC, The Car that Fought Back*, Interurban, Glendale, 1980

E. Carter, *Trams and Tramways*, Foyle, Taunton, 1961

J. Day, *London's Trams and Trolleybuses*, London Transport, London, 1977

C. Dunbar, *Buses, Trolleys & Trams*, Paul Hamlyn, London, 1967

G. Hilton, *The Cable Car in America*, Howell North, Berkeley, 1971

J. Joyce, *Tramways of the World*, Ian Allan, London, 1965

J. Larkins and B. Howard, *Romance of Australian Trams*, Rigby, Adelaide, 1978

I. Manning, *The Open Street*, Transit Australia, Sydney, 1991

J. McKay, *Tramways and Trolleys*, Princeton, Princeton, 1976

W. Middleton, *The Time of the Trolley*, Klambach, Milwaukee, 1967

J. Miller, *Fares Please!*, Dover, New York, 1941

J. White, *Horsecars, Cable Cars and Omnibuses*, Dover, New York, 1974

Specialist Journals

The Modern Tramway 1938-61

Modern Tramway 1962-91

Light Rail, 1992 onwards

Journal of the Light Rail Transit Association (Great Britain)

Tram Tracks 1946-49

included in *Railways of Australia*, 1949-51

Electric Traction, 1951-84

E T, 1985-86

Transit Australia, 1987 onwards

Journal of the Australian Electric Traction Association

Trolley Wire, 1952-55
Trolley Wire Review, 1956
Trolley Wire, 1957 onwards
Journal of the Australian Tramway Museums

Tramway Topics, 1962 onwards
Journal of the New Zealand Tramway Museums

Running Journal, 1964-73
Journal of the Tramway Museum Society of Victoria

Dreadnought, 1969-74
Journal of the Brisbane Tramway Museum Society

Australian material has also appeared on occasion in the American journals, *Headlights* and *Electric Lines*

Index